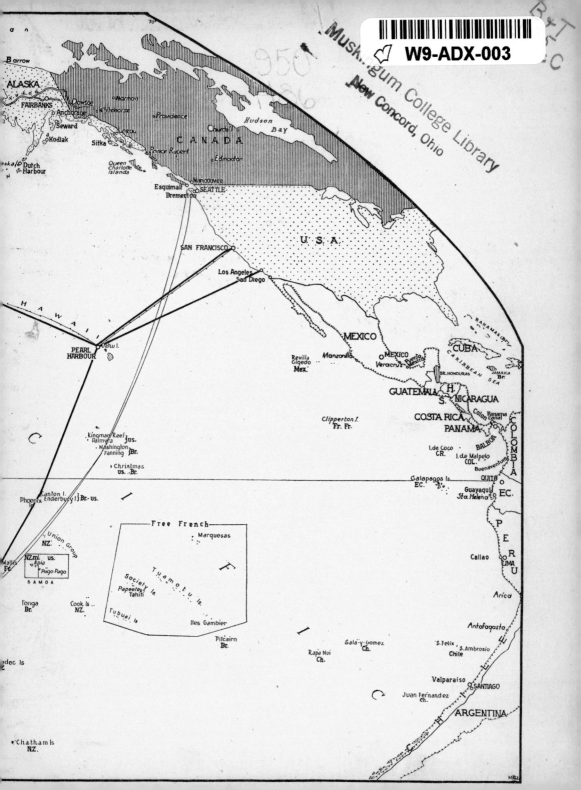

W9-ADX-003

AN ATLAS OF FAR EASTERN POLITICS

AN ATLAS OF
FAR EASTERN POLITICS

By

G. F. HUDSON and MARTHE RAJCHMAN

Enlarged Edition
With a Supplement for the Years 1938 to 1942 by
GEORGE E. TAYLOR

and additional maps by
MARTHE RAJCHMAN

Issued under the auspices of the
International Secretariat,
Institute of Pacific Relations, by

THE JOHN DAY COMPANY

NEW YORK
1942

FIRST PUBLISHED IN GREAT BRITAIN
BY FABER & FABER LTD. 1938

ENLARGED EDITION WITH SUPPLEMENT FOR THE YEARS 1938 TO 1942
FIRST PUBLISHED IN THE UNITED STATES 1942

Copyright, 1942, by the
Secretariat, Institute of Pacific Relations

PRINTED IN THE UNITED STATES OF AMERICA
BY THE HADDON CRAFTSMEN, INC., CAMDEN, N. J.

PREFACE

In sponsoring the publication in the United States of this enlarged edition of *An Atlas of Far Eastern Politics* the Secretariat of the Institute of Pacific Relations has been mainly concerned to make available to North American readers a book which has never had the distribution it deserved in the United States and one which recent dramatic developments in the Far East have made even more important than when it was first published in England.

Though surprisingly little of the earlier edition has been rendered out of date by the march of events, it has seemed desirable to add a supplement dealing particularly with the course of the Sino-Japanese war since 1938 and with the impact which the European war has had upon the whole Far Eastern scene. This supplement, written by Professor George E. Taylor, head of the Far Eastern Department at the University of Washington and author of *The Struggle for North China*, has been prepared quite independently and without consultation with Mr. Hudson. Considerations of time and space have made it impossible to model the supplement exactly upon the earlier chapters of the *Atlas* but it is hoped that the principal broad tendencies of the past three and a half years have been reasonably well covered. It has not been possible to include an account of the reactions in

7

PREFACE

the Far East to the current struggle between Nazi Germany and the Soviet Union.

The sudden attack by Japan against Hawaii, the Philippines and Malaya on December 7 followed by the German and Italian declarations of war against the United States finally brought the Far East and America into another world war. That war will change many of the facts and problems discussed herein, but for the present the need for such a book is immensely increased and it has therefore been decided to issue it without attempting revisions to meet the current war developments.

Though the present edition is issued under the auspices of the Secretariat of the Institute of Pacific Relations, neither the Secretariat nor any of the Institute's national councils accepts responsibility for statements of fact or opinion in the book or for its maps. The authors alone are responsible for both text and maps.

W. L. HOLLAND
Research Secretary

New York
March 1, 1942

CONTENTS

Mar '43

9

MAPS

MAPS

AN ATLAS OF FAR EASTERN POLITICS

Chapter I

THE APPROACHES TO THE FAR EAST

There have been in history three ways of approach to the region of the world known as the Far East: the first, by sea from the Indian Ocean; the second, overland from the countries of the Middle East; and the third, across the Pacific from North or South America.

The trans-Pacific approach belongs to modern times; it dates only from the voyage of Magellan in 1519. The Polynesians navigated vast expanses of the Pacific in outrigger canoes, but there is no evidence that they ever jumped the gaps that separate Hawaii and Easter Island from the Americas. Disabled Japanese junks have occasionally been carried by wind and current to the coast of California, but no definite knowledge of America seems to have come to Asia by such accidents. The pre-Columbian natives of the New World were not seafarers, and the close proximity of North America and Asia at the Bering Strait, however important for the peopling of the Americas with human stock, belongs to a zone too remote from the areas of old civilization to have significance in history. It may be said without considerable qualification that up to the sixteenth century of our era the Pacific Ocean imposed an absolute limit to human intercourse east of Asia.

15

THE APPROACHES TO THE FAR EAST

The approaches by sea and land from the Middle East, on the other hand, have been in use from remote antiquity, and an account of them must reveal the natural boundaries of the Far Eastern region, for it is just the main obstacles to communication with the farther parts of Asia which determine the most suitable limits for the three conventional divisions of the continent into Near, Middle and Far East. It is always possible, of course, to divide an area of the earth's surface merely according to a scale of remoteness, but such a regional partition should have more of geographical significance than this, and the three degrees of removal which we recognize in viewing Asia from Europe actually do correspond to definable natural areas.

Leaving out of account the Arctic littoral, Asia has three coastlines: to the west, the Mediterranean and Black Sea, to the south, the Indian Ocean, and to the east, the Pacific. Before the making of the canal, the isthmus of Suez barred any access for shipping from the Mediterranean to the Indian Ocean, and even now it remains a very definite dividing line. From the Indian Ocean to the Pacific there is a continuous natural seaway, but the Malay Peninsula, reaching south to within two degrees of the Equator, makes a very sharp corner at the southeastern extremity of Asia, and Singapore is no less of a boundary than Suez. The three Asiatic coastlines are thus clearly separated, and their hinterlands may be identified with the three regions of the East; by this criterion the Near East includes Turkey and Syria (with Egypt), the Middle East, Arabia, Iraq, Iran and India, and the Far East, Indo-China and China.

These divisions by relation to coastline would not, however, have so much significance if they did not correspond to two well-marked insulating barriers inland. The Ararat highlands and the Hamad (Syrian desert) intervene between the Mediterranean and Persian Gulf lands, and formerly set an eastward limit to that Mediterranean-centered political creation, the Roman empire. Similarly, a vast mountain system comprising the Pamirs-Tibet and Yunnan-Burma highlands shuts off China from India and Iran, the mountains being reinforced to the north of Tibet by the deserts of Sinkiang. These two great ramparts of natural obstruction may be regarded as fixing the confines of the Near, Middle and Far Eastern regions.

The Pamirs-Burma mountain system affords by far the more impervious barrier of the two, and accounts for the high degree of isolation which was the condition of Far Eastern history until quite recently. Though the isolation of the Far East has often been exaggerated, it remains true that China has been in the past more secluded from cultural contact and interaction with an outer world than any section of the region extending from Spain to Bengal; the history of China is more self-contained than that of India, Persia, Greece or Western Europe. The Achaemenid kings of ancient Persia, Alexander the Great and the Arab Caliphs all bridged the gap between Near and Middle East and ruled from the shores of the Mediterranean to the Pamirs, but none of them passed the Pamirs and penetrated to China; nor did any Indian kingdom extend its sway beyond the Himalayas or east of the Salween. Buddhism was propagated from India throughout the Far East, but it never displaced the traditional native religion of China; Islam also reached China, but it never created there a new epoch of history as it did in India. The snows of Sarikol and the Kum Tagh sands repelled the temporal power of Persepolis or Baghdad and weakened the impact of those spiritual forces which they could not forbid.

THE APPROACHES TO THE FAR EAST

By longitude Tibet and Sinkiang, lying north of the Ganges plain, should be comprised within the Middle East, but the course of history which has made them to this day—at least nominally—parts of China, corresponds to a strong geographical predisposition; they are more accessible from the east than from the south or west, though just lately, since the construction of the Turksib railway, the gravitational pull of the Soviet Union has been very strong in Sinkiang. From the great peak of Khan Tengri (23,620 feet) in the T'ien-shan southwest of Kulja round to the great gorge by which the Dihong cuts its way down from Tibet to become the Brahmaputra in the plains of Assam, the formal frontier of China follows the line of the most tremendous mountain rampart in the world. The T'ien-shan, the Pamirs, the Karakorum and the Himalayas are all mountain ranges on a grand scale, and the last-named is backed by the vast plateau of Tibet, a country where many tens of thousands of square miles lie higher than the summit of Mont Blanc. On these upper levels the way for caravans has always been arduous in the extreme; Marco Polo tells of the forty days' journey on the high Pamirs, where "in all this way you shall come to no town, nor habitation, nor grass, and therefore it is needful for those that do travel that way to carry with them provision and victuals for themselves and their horses."

It is possible to avoid the high mountains by going to the north of the T'ien-shan and then southeast to China *via* Hami. There is a clear way from west to east across Asia through the gap between the T'ien-shan and the mountains of the Altai system. This way went the caravan route from the Sea of Azov to Peiping described by Pegolotti in the fourteenth century, and this way runs the road from the Turksib railway to Lanchow by which Russian munitions are supplied to China in the present war. But for access to China from India or Persia such a route has always meant a long detour added onto a distance already excessive for commerce before the age of mechanical transport. For an approach from the direction of the lower Volga it was more convenient, but, whatever its natural advantages, it has been at most times in history rendered extremely difficult for trade or travel by the nomadic barbarism of the steppes through which it passes. The same applies in an even greater degree to the open country to the north of the Altai; here there could be no question of a route from Indian or Mediterranean countries to the Far East, and the opening of trans-Asian communications in such high latitudes depended on the development of Russia and her expansion eastward through Siberia—it dates, therefore, only from the seventeenth century.

Turning from the north to the south of the great central mountain block of Asia, we find obstruction of a somewhat different kind, but no less formidable. From the southeastern corner of the Tibetan plateau mountain ranges splay out toward the south, reaching the sea in Tenasserim, where the Malay Peninsula juts out from the land-mass of Indo-China. These mountains diminish rapidly in height from north to south—though there are large areas over 10,000 feet as far south as lat. 25°—and on this border there are no perils from blizzard and avalanche or complications of desert and nomadic marauders. But an exceptionally high annual rainfall—the world's record of 424 inches average is held by Cherrapunji in the Khasi hills in Assam—clothes the hill tracts facing the Bay of Bengal with dense tropical vegetation, which makes them hardly less difficult to traverse than the loftier heights of the Pamirs or

Himalayas. Nor has the human population been more favorable to economic and cultural contacts of a high order than it has in the steppe and alpine grasslands of Central Asia. An environment of mountain forests has kept a wide region in the interior of Indo-China in various stages of primitive culture more or less impervious to influences from areas of higher civilization to west, east and south; the Naga, Mishmi, Kachin and Wa tribes were head-hunters until yesterday, and the more civilized Shans and Karens, forming numerous petty principalities in their hill-girt valleys, have always stoutly resisted incorporation in any large, centralized state.

With such obstacles to overland communication between the Middle and Far East, it might seem, nevertheless, that the continuous seaway from the Indian Ocean into the Pacific would afford a sufficiently close contact. Yet the Malay Peninsula has been up to modern times a strong factor of separation, for not only did it mean a long, roundabout voyage from the Bay of Bengal to the South China Sea, but it diverted maritime traffic into waters where piracy used to flourish with peculiar vigor. Malaya, Sumatra and Borneo, with their numerous adjacent small islands, lying within the zone of equatorial rain forest, always remained a region of backward culture, the inhabitants of which preferred freebooting to regular trade, so that shipping on the way between India and China was at all times in hazard. With the arrival of gun-armed European ships in the seas round Malaya the pirate proa met more than its match, but in earlier centuries the development of commerce in these waters was seriously impeded by a piracy too ubiquitous and elusive ever to be suppressed. Even after Malacca had grown into a great emporium for trade from Java and the Moluccas, as well as from

Siam and China, the institutions of orderly economic life were little in evidence, and the Italian traveler Varthema, who visited Malacca in 1506, complains that "one cannot walk about at night here, because people are killed like dogs, and the merchants who come sleep on their ships. . . . The king has a governor to administer justice for foreigners, but the people of the country take the law into their own hands, and they are the worst race that was ever created on earth."

In view of the length and dangers of the voyage through the Straits of Malacca and round Malaya, trade tended to make use of a portage across the isthmus of Kra, renouncing the advantages of continuous voyage, but reducing the risks from piracy. The isthmus of Kra appears to have been the main center for the diffusion of Indian influences in Indo-China during the early centuries of our era,[1] and later a route from Bangkok to Tenasserim was much in use for the export of Chinese porcelain to Islamic countries—a trade well attested by the quantities of broken wares recovered from the earth in this area.

With or without the Kra short cut, however, the "southeast passage" failed throughout ancient and medieval times to attain primacy as a means of access to the Far East, and the overland routes through Sinkiang, in spite of their difficulties, retained most of the traffic there was. The main trans-Asian caravan route in the second century A.D. ran from Antioch in Syria to Ctesiphon (on the Tigris below Baghdad) and thence by the modern Hamadan, Damghan, Merv, Balkh and the Pamir passes to Tashkurgan in Sarikol, where there was a mart for Chinese raw silk, which was brought from China Proper through Sin-

[1] The Khmer culture of Cambodia, represented by the famous ruins of Angkor, thus received its initial stimulus.

kiang either by the route to the north of the Taklamakan desert (Anhsi-Hami-Turfan-Karashar-Kuchar-Akus-Kashgar) or by that to the south of it (Anhsi-Tunhuang-Charkhlik-Charchan-Keriya-Khotan-Yarkand). No road to the north of the T'ien-shan appears to have been used in that period, but later on a trade route from the Black Sea to Samarkand *via* Astrakhan and Khiva, which became important from the sixth century onward, was extended to China by way of Kulja, Urumchi[1] and Hami. In the time of Marco Polo both the trans-Pamir and Kulja-Urumchi routes were in use, corresponding to lines of approach to China from south and north of the Caspian respectively; Marco himself, coming through Persia, traveled by Kashgar, Khotan and Charchan, but the elder Polos came from Sarai on the Volga to Bokhara, and they probably went on by Kulja.

From India and from the Bay of Bengal there were two direct overland routes to China: one across the Himalayas and Tibet *via* Lhasa, and the other by Burma and Yunnan. So great were the disadvantages, however, of both these ways that the main lines of communication between India and China, during the period when Buddhism was propagated from India all over the Far East, were through Sinkiang. From Kashmir there was always the road to Kashgar by Hunza and the Mintaka pass (15,450 feet), or the Balkh-Kashgar road could be reached further west *via* Chitral or Kabul—a roundabout way of getting from the Ganges to the Yellow River, but the best available in pre-modern conditions of travel.

After the arrival of European shipping in the Indian Ocean with the voyage of Vasco da Gama in 1498, the sea route round Malaya was opened up more than ever before, and became by

[1] Now officially Tihwa, but better known by its old name.

far the most important approach to the Far East. The traditional overland routes fell into decline, and, in particular, the old Khotan-Charchan route was almost completely abandoned. On the other hand, the last four centuries have seen the development by Western powers of two new lines of approach: the trans-Siberian and trans-Pacific.

The Russians, pressing eastward to the north of the Altai, reached Lake Baikal early in the seventeenth century and opened trade with China across Mongolia along the route Irkutsk-Kiakhta-Urga-Peiping. But when in the last decade of the nineteenth century the building of a transcontinental railway was undertaken by Russia, it was decided to carry it, not across the Gobi to Peiping and Tientsin, but to the most southerly Russian port on the Pacific. The political situation in 1896 having enabled the Russians to get permission from China to build the line through Manchuria, it became possible to approach China overland from Russia without having to cross either high mountains or deserts. The trans-Siberian was eventually linked with the Chinese railway system by the connection Harbin-Mukden-Peiping, entering China not from the northwest or north, but from the *northeast*. The Russians have had plans ever since the 'nineties for a short-cut line from the Trans-Siberian to China Proper *via* Urga or Hami, but no such railway has yet been built, though there is now a line as far as Urga (Ulan Bator, the capital of Outer Mongolia).

The approach to Asia across the Pacific dates only, as has been already pointed out, from Magellan's voyage in 1519. Up to about 1850 ships came from the direction of Cape Horn or the Magellan Straits, having sailed round South America from Europe or New England; or they came from the Pacific ports of

THE APPROACHES TO THE FAR EAST

Latin America, Mexico being the most northerly region of European settlement on the Pacific coast. Then, with the rapid growth of San Francisco as a port of the U.S.A. from 1848 onward, shipping began to sail thence almost due west—actually with a slant southward through six degrees of latitude—to Shanghai, which had been first opened to foreign trade in 1842. Japan, which had hitherto held place as the far end of the Far East, the Cipangu which Marco Polo heard of but never reached, lay in the path of the new oceanic trade route, and it was the Americans coming across the Pacific, not the Europeans approaching from the south, who in 1853 compelled the self-secluded Japanese to enter into relations with the outer world.

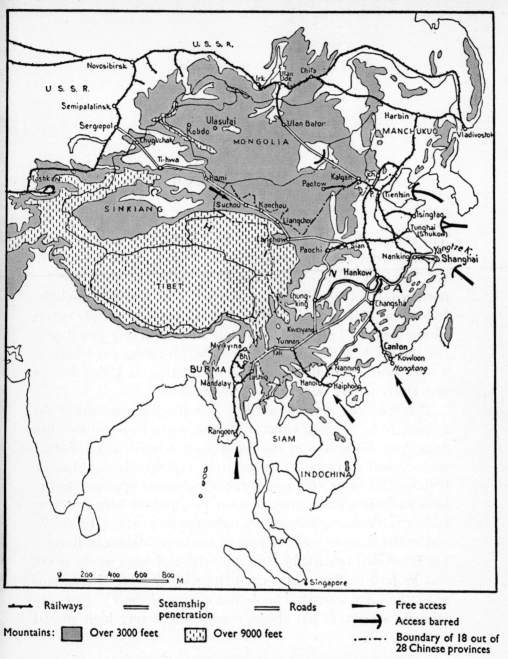

1. WAYS OF ACCESS TO CHINA (MODERN)

Railways   Steamship penetration   Roads   Free access

Access barred

Mountains: Over 3000 feet   Over 9000 feet   Boundary of 18 out of 28 Chinese provinces

0 200 400 600 800 M

Chapter II

LANDS AND PEOPLES

The region of the Far East may be divided into three zones: a southern zone extending from lat. 10° south of the Equator to 20° north of it, a middle one from 20°N. to 40°N., and a northern from 40°N. to the Arctic. The southern includes Indonesia, Malaya and most of Indo-China, the middle covers China Proper, Tibet and the main areas of Korea and Japan, and the northern comprises Manchuria, Mongolia and Siberia—a vast continental area which in its relation to China Proper may conveniently be termed the Northland.

The southern zone of the Far East lies entirely within the tropics. It includes an equatorial zone, extending to about five degrees on both sides of the Equator, in which there is hardly any seasonal variation of temperature or rainfall; this climatic belt appears to be very unfavorable to human progress, and to such environmental influence must be attributed the fact that Indian civilization, diffused over the nearer parts of Indonesia and Indo-China, never took root in Sumatra, Malaya or Borneo, but flourished remarkably in Cambodia and Siam to the north and in Java to the south—countries with definite alternations of wet and dry seasons. The southern zone of the Far East contains no deserts; it has almost everywhere a very high annual

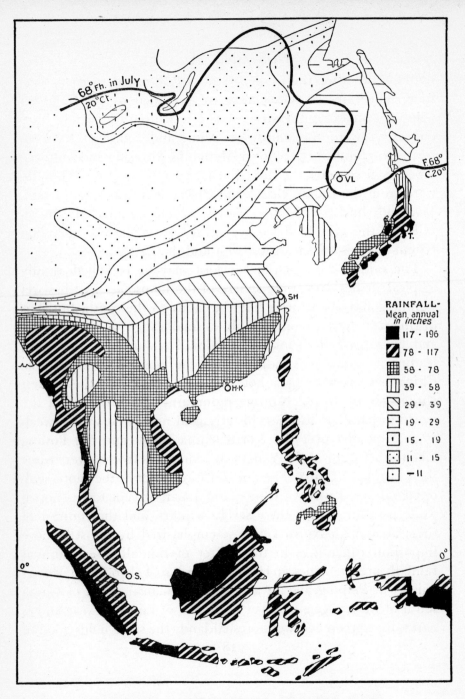

68° Fh. in July
20° Ct.

F.68°
C.20°

○ VL

T.

○ SH

RAINFALL-
Mean annual
in inches

	117 - 196
	78 - 117
	58 - 78
	39 - 58
	29 - 39
	19 - 29
	15 - 19
	11 - 15
	- 11

○ H·K

○ S.

0°

0°

2. CLIMATIC REGIONS OF THE FAR EAST

rainfall and is for the most part heavily forested in its natural
state. The rains of Indo-China are provided by the monsoon
wind system of southeastern Asia. In winter the winds blow
outward toward the southwest, south and southeast from an
intense high-pressure belt over Mongolia, Sinkiang and southern
Siberia; in summer the direction is reversed and they blow in-
ward from the Indian Ocean and China Seas as bearers of rain.
Java and the Lesser Sunda Islands, which are affected climati-
cally by the arid land surface of Australia, have a monsoon
system of their own with wet west and dry east winds.

The middle zone of the Far East may be reckoned as sub-
tropical; it lies within the sphere of the monsoons, and has wet
summers and dry winters like the lands to the south, but it is
distinguished by a considerable annual range of temperature
and by a marked shrinking of rainfall toward the northwest,
leading to sub-arid conditions on the borders of Mongolia.
China has everywhere a hot summer, but it has the coldest
winter—south to the Nanling mountains—for any part of the
world in parallel latitudes; bitterly cold northwest winds sweep
from Mongolia over the North China Plain, and the Poyang
lake to the south of the Yangtse is sometimes frozen over below
the latitude of Cairo. The South China littoral, the more shel-
tered valleys of western China, and Japan, except for its northwestern coasts, escape these severe winters, and the contrast of
these areas with North China is emphasized by the still more
important differences in the matter of rainfall. Mean annual
rainfalls are 85 inches at Hongkong, 58 at Tokyo, 45 at Shanghai, 25 at Peiping and 14 at Taiyuan (Shansi). Most of China
south of the Yangtse has over 50 inches of rain in a year and is
naturally a green and well-forested land; the same holds good of

Japan, where luxuriant timber covers nearly all the ground that is not under cultivation. North China, on the other hand, is a region of comparatively low rainfall, declining below 10 inches in parts of Kansu; in good years the rains are sufficient for agriculture, but they often fail to reach the necessary minimum and the resulting crop failures produce famine. Much of North China is now practically treeless; this is partly due to artificial deforestation—always terribly effective in such marginal lands —but the country, even in early times, can only have been lightly timbered as compared with South China, Indo-China or Japan. Its character predestined it to be the original seat of the great independent civilization of the Far East, for under neolithic cultural conditions the zone of decisive initial progress was the sub-tropical, sub-arid, the grade between the well-watered forest land and the steppe or desert. Indian civilization arose in the dry lands of Sind and the Punjab, and only later spread over the rain-favored plains of the Ganges; similarly, Chinese civilization arose in the basin of the Yellow River and had attained there a high level more than a thousand years before we find evidence of any such development in the valleys of the Yangtse, the Si-kiang or the Mekong.

The contrast between the Yellow River and Yangtse lands in the time of the Han dynasty (206 B.C.—A.D. 221) was noted by the Chinese historian Ssu-ma Ch'ien, who describes the latter as a "large territory sparsely populated, where people eat rice and drink fish soup; where land is tilled with fire and hoed with water; where people collect fruits and shellfish for food and enjoy self-sufficiency without commerce. The region is fertile and suffers no famine. Hence the people are lazy and poor and do not bother to accumulate wealth; south of the Yangtse and the Hwai there are neither hungry nor frozen people, nor a family which owns a thousand gold."[1] Yet the Yangtse valley came in course of time to be no less intensively cultivated and densely peopled than the old China of the Yellow River, and this result was brought about by colonization from the north; the natural fertility of the south country was made to yield its wealth to a technique of agriculture developed under more arduous conditions.

The land areas of the southern and middle zones of the Far East are everywhere capable of cultivation except for mountainous tracts and the higher plateaux of Tibet. In the third zone, however, we come to an immense region over by far the greater part of which agriculture is forbidden either by aridity or frigidity of climate. The Northland, extending from the Great Wall of China to the Arctic Ocean, is divisible into three sub-zones: one of steppe and desert in the forties of latitude, a second, of forest (generally sparse east of the Yenisei), and a third, of treeless "tundra" above the Arctic Circle. Of the steppe region only the fringes can be cultivated, but the whole provides pasture for animals and has thus been traditionally the domain of horse-riding, tent-dwelling, milk-sustained herdsmen, who represent a culture diametrically opposed to that of the sedentary, agricultural Chinese. These nomads have always been the neighbors of China to the north, and until recently were one of the main factors in Chinese history.

Before the coming of the Russians regular agriculture in the Northland was confined to the piedmont oases of Sinkiang and the pale of Chinese settlement in southern Manchuria. The belt

[1] Ssu-ma Ch'ien, *chüan* 102. Quoted by Ch'ao-ting Chi, *Key Economic Areas in Chinese History*, p. 98.

of arable land along the present Trans-Siberian railway to the north of Mongolia and in northern Manchuria remained wilderness, being cut off from Chinese colonization or influence by nomad-infested steppe and lacking river communication with the south—the fact that all the great rivers of northern Asia flow either to the Arctic Ocean (the Ob, Yenisei and Lena) or to the northerly Okhotsk Sea (the Amur) has contributed much to the historic isolation of Siberia. Up to the middle of the seventeenth century there was nothing in northeastern Asia above the forty-fifth parallel of latitude except a barbarism with gradations from the hunting-and-fishing economy of the Chukchis and Ghilaks through the reindeer-keeping of the Yakuts and Tungus to the horse-and-cattle nomadism of the Mongols.

The Northland Pacific littoral has a character of its own which is extremely adverse to human habitation. This region combines the intense cold of the Siberian winter with a chilly, wet summer unfavorable either for agriculture or stock-raising. East of the Stanovoi mountains the northern limit of cereals descends to about the latitude of Paris, and at Vladivostok in the parallel of Marseilles the sea freezes for four months in the year. The climatic conditions closely resemble those of Labrador in similar latitudes on the east coast of North America, and even Soviet planning has not so far made much out of this territory. In former times Possiet Bay was the northern limit for shipping, Chinese, Japanese or Korean, and no attempt was ever made to colonize the coasts beyond.

Turning from environment and basic economic types to ethnography, we find that the whole of the southern and middle zones of the Far East, with the exception of Korea and Japan, is occupied by peoples belonging to three great linguistic families:

NOTE ON MAP 3

This map is intended to indicate the distribution of the principal ethnic types without reference to density of population. For the relative density of population in the provinces of China Proper and Manchuria, see maps 18 and 24.

The Tibetans, Turks, Mongols and Tungus occupy large areas on the map, but with very low density; the Chinese and Russian areas, on the other hand, are generally of high density, and the Chinese and Russians often form the urban population in regions where the native peoples still predominate in the open country. Thus all the towns of Siberia may be counted as Russian and those of the Miao, Shan and Lolo districts of the west and southwest of China as Chinese.

32

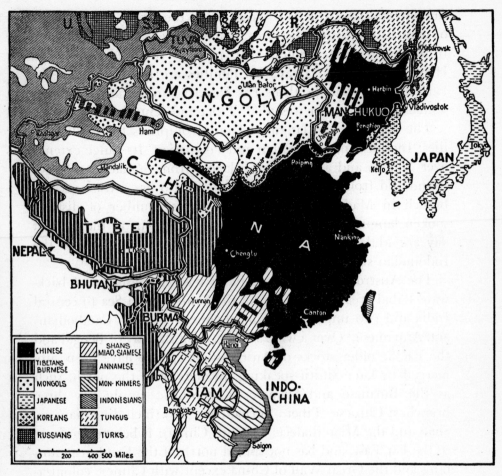

3. ETHNOGRAPHY OF THE FAR EAST

the Austronesian, the Austroasiatic and the Sinitic. It is worthy of note, as indicating the separateness of the Far Eastern region from very remote times, that neither the Indo-European, Hamito-Semitic nor Dravidian families are represented in the Far East, and that the three Far Eastern families are not represented in Asia farther west than Tibet and central India.

The Austronesian language family comprises three sub-families: Indonesian, Melanesian and Polynesian. Its range extends over Malaya and all the archipelagoes from Sumatra to Easter Island and from Timor to Formosa; it also has a trans-oceanic branch in Madagascar. It covers a large number of distinct spoken languages, of which the most important at the present day are Malay, Javanese, Sundanese and Tagalog—all of the Indonesian sub-family.

The Austroasiatic group includes several languages of backward tribal areas scattered from the South China Sea to central India and two important living tongues—Khmer (Cambodian) and Annamese.[1] Over a wide area between the Bay of Bengal and the Pacific older stocks of Austroasiatic speech have been submerged by later Sinitic-speaking invaders from the north, such as the Burmese and Siamese. The Sinitic family has three branches: Chinese, Tibeto-Burman and Tai (including Siamese, Shan and the Miao dialects of South China); it belongs entirely to the Far East, and has not spread north of the Kunlun mountains and the Great Wall of China except with Chinese colonization in historic times.

The greater part of the Northland was held before the arrival

---

[1] Annamese is classified by some with the Tai group of the Sinitic family. See, however, J. Przyluski, *Langues austroasiatiques* in *Les Langues du monde*, ed. A. Meillet and M. Cohen, pp. 395-8.

of the Russians by tongues of the Altaian family, classifiable into Turkish, Mongol and Tungusic branches. This language group, owing to its association with nomadism, is very widely spread; its range extends to the Mediterranean (Turkey), to the Arctic Ocean (the Yakuts) and to the Pacific (the Tungus), but the total of its speakers is small outside the settled communities of Turkey, Azerbaijan and Turkestan.

Beyond the foregoing threefold classification of Far Eastern languages fall Korean, Japanese and certain tribal languages of the extreme northeast of Siberia and the Primorsk, the affinities of which have not yet been discovered.[1] The geographical distribution of these forms of speech on the farthest rim of Asia suggests that they are survivals comparable to Basque in Europe.

On such ethnic foundations cultural tradition and political state-making have in course of time created unities and differences from which nationalities in the modern sense of the word have been, or are being, formed. Besides the two big indigenous nations of the Far East, the Chinese and the Japanese, there are today about a dozen lesser nationalities which have to be taken into account, and in addition, a large number of human beings living in tribal or petty local units and eluding any "national" classification.

By cultural tradition older than the arrival of Europeans the peoples of the Far East—leaving out of account the more primitive tribal elements—belong to three different domains of civilization: the Chinese, the Indian and the Islamic. The first of

[1] It is held by some that Japanese is related to the Indonesian group and therefore to the Austronesian family of languages, but there is so far no consensus of opinion on the matter among philologists.

these is native to the Far East, whereas the other two are intrusive from the west.

Chinese civilization, having grown up in the basin of the Yellow River, extended its domain in two ways: through colonization by the Chinese themselves and through the reception of Chinese culture by non-Chinese peoples. The former type of expansion prevailed as far south as Hainan and formed the modern China Proper, including the Yangtse and Si-kiang basins; the latter kind brought Annam, Korea and Japan within the Chinese cultural sphere, all these three countries adopting classical literary Chinese as the language of education and learning.

Indian culture from about the beginning of our era penetrated by colonization and influenced Indo-China (except Annam) and the nearer parts of Indonesia. The traditional culture of Siam and Cambodia is thus affiliated, but in Malaya and Indonesia the Hindu-Buddhist influence was superseded by Islam in the fourteenth and fifteenth centuries and now survives only in Bali. In another direction Indian cultural expansion was even more far-reaching; from the first century A.D. Buddhism was transmitted to China along the silk-trading caravan routes through Sinkiang, and through China it reached also Korea and Japan. Within the sphere of the Chinese literary tradition, however, the Indian religion was always a subsidiary element—except for a while in Japan. More profound was the effect of Buddhism in Tibet, where it assumed the special form known as lamaism and dominated the whole life of the country. From Tibet Lama-Buddhism spread northeastward to Mongolia, and both in Tibet and Mongolia modern nationalist feeling has its roots in a national "church," even though it is anti-clerical in tendency.

Following in the wake of India's spiritual expansion, Islam, spreading from Arabia and Iran, likewise reached the Far East on two courses, one to the south and the other to the north. Across the Indian Ocean Arab traders and adventurers propagated their faith among the Malays of Sumatra, who carried it to other parts of Indonesia. The Hindu power in Java was destroyed by the capture of Madjopait in 1478 and Java became entirely Mohammedan. Islam was spread eastward as far as Mindanao, Ceram and Timor, but everywhere except in Java prevailed only in coastal districts, the inland tribes retaining their primitive paganism.

In Central Asia the Turki-speaking people of Sinkiang were converted to Islam as were their kinsmen to the west of the Pamirs. The line between Moslem and Buddhist now corresponds almost exactly to the linguistic division of Turk and Mongol. Further, Islam, cutting across the line of Buddhist expansion from Tibet to Mongolia, established itself in northwest China and created the numerous Chinese-speaking Moslem community known as Tungans, who can hardly be counted as a separate nationality, but form a very distinct and centrifugal section of the Chinese people.

To these formative factors of cultural inheritance must be added, as constituents of nationality, historical traditions of political sovereignty and state-making. In China there is the great tradition of the "Middle Kingdom" and of the Son of Heaven, who before 1860 could not recognize any other earthly monarch as his equal. In Japan there is the national sovereign of divine descent, who, whatever the chaos of Japanese internal politics, was always the mystical talisman of the "Yamato race." Korea, Annam, Cambodia and Siam have their traditions of strong, organized national kingdoms. The Mongols derive an intense racial pride from the memory of the empire of Genghiz Khan, and the Tibetans have their long-established sovereignty of the holy Dalai Lama. In Indonesia there is still the memory of the old Javanese empire of Mataram. These historical continuities serve as nuclei for modern national feeling, even when the nationalism is anti-monarchical and destructive of traditional culture; though popular nationalism and its jargon are recent innovations, the main lines of nationality which now exist were already drawn before Europeans ever reached the Far East. To the old ethno-political units, however, the age of European ascendency has added two more: the Russian, which is the product of immigration from Europe, and the Filipino, which is a creation of Spanish colonialism.

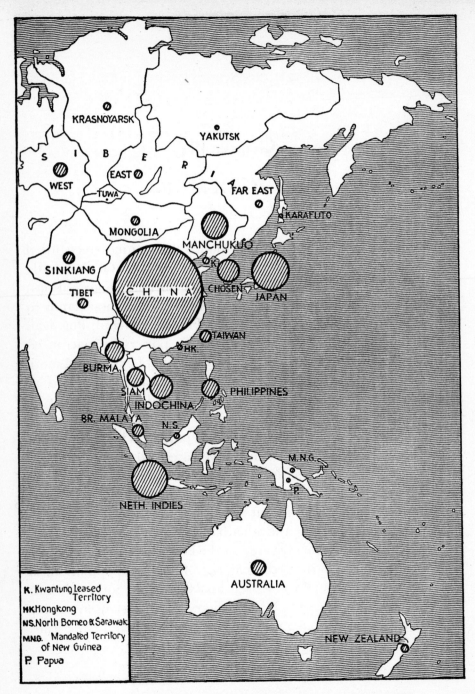

K. Kwantung Leased Territory
HK Hongkong
NS. North Borneo & Sarawak
MNG. Mandated Territory of New Guinea
P. Papua

4. POPULATIONS OF FAR EASTERN COUNTRIES

Chapter III

THE WESTERNERS

There are today, excluding Manchukuo, nine recognized
sovereignties within the confines of the Far East. Of these only
three—China, Japan and Siam—belong to indigenous nations;
the rest are held by "Western" nations with their homelands in
Europe or North America—Britain, France, Holland, Portugal,
the U.S.A. and the U.S.S.R. All these six powers have acquired
their territories in the Far East by some kind of expansion, more
or less violent, since a Portuguese squadron first arrived at
Malacca in 1509. In the sequel, however, a distinction must be
drawn between the Far Eastern lands of the Soviet Union and
the "possessions" of the other Western powers. The latter are in
every case imperial ascendencies over areas already well populated, and the ruling nations are represented by mere handfuls
of administrators, soldiers, capitalist entrepreneurs and techni-
cians, who form insignificant minorities among the native inhabitants; in Siberia, on the other hand, the Russians have settled
on land previously uncultivated, as the English have in Canada or
Australia, and form the great majority of the total population, so
that Russian nationality, as well as Russian (or Soviet Union)
state power, has been established there. The Russians are today
a Far Eastern nation in a way the British, French and Americans

are not, though their actual numbers are small to the east of the Yenisei, and their position as a Great Power is based on their wealth of population and resources in Europe and West Siberia.

The history of European commercial and imperial expansion in the Far East begins in 1509, when a Portuguese squadron under Sequiera arrived at Malacca to open trade eleven years after Vasco da Gama had first reached India round the Cape of Good Hope. The usual disputes having arisen, Albuquerque, the Portuguese Captain-General of the Indies, attacked and captured Malacca in 1511. The Portuguese thus acquired a monopoly of the lucrative trade in spices from the Moluccas; to complete their control they annexed the Moluccas in 1522 and held them until 1583, when they were driven out by a rebellion of the natives. Their principal rivals in these waters in the early days were the Spanish, who crossed the Pacific from Mexico and tried to break the Portuguese hold on the Moluccas; failing in this, the Spanish went farther north and conquered the group of islands which they named the Philippines in honor of King Philip II. From Malacca the Portuguese had meanwhile opened up trade with China and Japan, and in China they were granted, in return for services in the suppression of piracy, a lease for a settlement at Macao in 1557. Macao became a Portuguese stronghold and was never lost, though it always remained nominally Chinese territory until it was formally annexed by Portugal in 1845.

With the beginning of the seventeenth century the Dutch and the English began to make their presence felt in Indonesia. The Dutch in 1619 captured Jacatra in Java and made it their Far Eastern base under the name of Batavia; in 1642 they also took Malacca from the Portuguese, and the latter were finally eliminated from the Archipelago except for a foothold on the island of Timor, the eastern half of which still belongs to them. The English, who tended more and more to concentrate their attention on India, likewise gave way to the Dutch after a period of rivalry. The Spanish, however, continued to hold the Philippines.

Dutch rule was strongly established in Java and the Moluccas; elsewhere in the islands their control was slight, and numerous petty rajas and sultans retained a somewhat diminished independence. The Dutch secured the monopoly of cloves by exterminating the tree in every island but Amboyna, and when the spice trade ceased to be important, they turned their attention to coffee, which they produced in Java under a system of forced labor. To the north of Indonesia they obtained a monopoly of European trade with Japan from 1639—and retained it until 1854—and made a settlement on the island of Formosa, which they held until they were driven out by exiles from China, partisans of the fallen Ming dynasty, in 1662.

Both China and Japan during the seventeenth and eighteenth centuries adopted a policy of restricting foreign trade and residence to particular ports, partly because of their fear of the Catholic Christian missions, which had arrived with the traders and had had a very disturbing effect, especially in Japan; partly because of the desire of the governments to control the trade to their own fiscal advantage; and partly because Far Eastern countries had no system of international diplomatic intercourse and commercial law such as had been evolved in Europe. In China foreign trade was restricted by law to Canton after 1757; in Japan it was confined to Nagasaki, and there allowed only to the Chinese and the Dutch, from 1639. The European nations had to put up with this state of affairs, for up

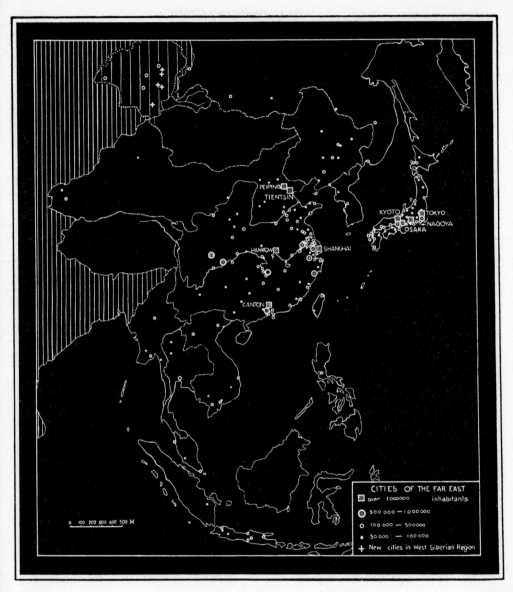

CITIES OF THE FAR EAST

over 1000000 inhabitants
500 000 — 1 000 000
100 000 — 500000
50 000 — 100 000
+ New cities in West Siberian Region

PEIPING
TIENTSIN
KYOTO TOKYO
OSAKA NAGOYA
HANKOW SHANGHAI
CANTON

0 100 200 300 400 500 M

5. CITIES OF THE FAR EAST

to the second quarter of the nineteenth century they were not in a position to apply coercion to China or Japan as they applied it to the petty principalities of Indonesia.

The Anglo-French wars from 1792 to 1815 brought English armed forces again into the Far East after Holland had fallen under the control of France. The English captured Malacca in 1795 and occupied Java in 1811; these and other Dutch possessions were restored to Holland in 1814, but in 1819 England acquired Singapore by cession from the Sultan of Johore and made it into a great commercial and strategic center.

In the final partition of Malaya and Indonesia among the Western powers, none of the native potentates was recognized as sovereign, and dominion was distributed in international law, that is, by treaties between Western powers, often in advance of conquest, or even of exploration. Large areas of Indonesia were not brought under any European authority until the present century; the conquest of Atjeh in northern Sumatra took some thirty years of campaigning. Today, however, it can be said that control by the recognized sovereign powers has been made effective throughout the whole region. The British hold all the Malay Peninsula south of Siam either by direct (Straits Settlements) or indirect (Protected Malay States) rule. The Dutch retain Java and the Lesser Sunda Islands, Sumatra, Borneo, Celebes and the Moluccas, with the exception of eastern Timor, which belongs to Portugal, and the northern part of Borneo, comprising British North Borneo and the British-protected states of Brunei and Sarawak.[1] The dominion of the Philippines

---

[1] Brunei was declared under British protection in 1888, Sarawak in 1890. The British protectorate over Atjeh in Sumatra was relinquished to the Dutch in 1872.

passed from Spain to the United States of America by the Spanish-American war of 1898, and at the same time the residue of the Spanish empire in the Pacific, consisting of the Pelew, Marianne and Caroline island groups in the ocean to the east of the Philippines, was ceded by Spain to Germany, to be taken from Germany by Japan in the war of 1914-18.

To the north of Malaya and Indonesia there were up to 1841 no European possessions except for the Portuguese leasehold of Macao and the Russian territory in the extreme north of the continent. The extent of the latter was defined by the Treaty of Nerchinsk, the first treaty ever signed by China with a European power, which was concluded in 1689. The Russians, whose empire in Asia had been founded by Yermak's capture of Sibir in 1581, had reached the Pacific coast at Okhotsk in 1647 and Lake Baikal in 1651; then they came into conflict with the Manchu-Chinese empire which controlled the basin of the Amur, and received a severe check. The Treaty of Nerchinsk fixed the Russo-Chinese border along the Stanovoi mountain range and the Uda river, leaving both banks of the Amur to China; this territorial settlement was not altered until 1858.

The Russian west-to-east advance through the far north of Asia did little to disturb the established order of things in the Far East during the seventeenth and eighteenth centuries, for it went on in a back-world of primitive tribes—Buryats, Yakuts and Tungus—beyond the ken of high politics. It meant, however, that for the first time in history there was a power in the Northland which was not founded on nomadism, and with the first settlements of Russian peasants east of the Yenisei a new nation came into being there.

45

THE WESTERNERS

The great European drive against China began with the Anglo-Chinese war of 1839 and it led to acquisitions in two categories: colonial and semi-colonial. The former kind, territorial gains in full sovereignty, included—

(1) Hongkong: the island ceded to Britain by China in 1841, Kowloon on the mainland added in 1860.

(2) French Indo-China: first annexations in 1862 in Cochin-China, protectorate over Cambodia in 1863, protectorate over Annam and Tongking (previously under Chinese suzerainty) recognized by China after Franco-Chinese war in 1885, Lao territory taken from Siam in 1893.

(3) Russian Far Eastern provinces: all country north of the Amur ceded by China to Russia in 1858, territory east of Usuri down to Korean border (including site of the future Vladivostok) ceded in 1860.

Besides these territories passing under European rule in full sovereignty, China was forced in 1898 to cede the following five districts under leasehold tenure, the occupying powers having complete rights of jurisdiction and military or naval use—

(1) Kiaochow: leased to Germany for 99 years, captured by Japanese 1914, restored to China 1922.

(2) Kwantung (Port Arthur and Dalny, now Ryojun and Dairen): renewable 25 years' lease to Russia, transferred to Japan by Treaty of Portsmouth 1905, lease prolonged to 99 years after ultimatum to China 1915.

(3) Weihaiwei: leased to Britain for "as long as Russia shall remain in occupation of Port Arthur," restored to China 1930.

(4) Hongkong New Territory, consisting of "all the land re-

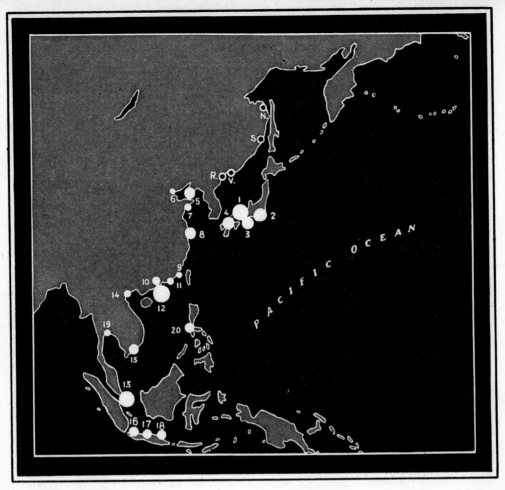

1 Kobe ⎤	12 Hongkong ⎤ British Colonies
2 Yokohama ⎥	13 Singapore ⎦
3 Osaka ⎬ Japan	14 Haiphong ⎤ French Colonies
4 Moji ⎥	15 Saigon ⎦
5 Dairen ⎦	16 Batavia ⎤
6 Tientsin ⎤	17 Semarang ⎬ Dutch Colonies
7 Tsingtao ⎥	18 Soerabaya ⎦
8 Shanghai ⎬ China	19 Bangkok, Siam
9 Amoy ⎥	20 Manila, Philippines
10 Canton ⎥	
11 Swatow ⎦	

Minimum shown: 1,000,000 tons of overseas traffic. Vladivostok (V), Sovetskaya (S). Nikolaevsk (N) and Rashin (R) fall short of this minimum, but are shown as a matter of interest.

6. PORTS OF THE FAR EAST

quired for the military defense of Hongkong": leased to Britain for 99 years.

(5) Kwangchow: leased to France for 99 years.

The leased territories were, and are, to all intents and purposes the colonial possessions of the states holding them. There is, however, another category of foreign treaty or customary rights in China which are definitely encroachments on Chinese sovereignty without conferring a generalized territorial control; these include the autonomous foreign "concessions" and settlements, the foreign gunboats on inland waters, the Legation guards at Peiping and garrisons in the Peiping-Tientsin area, and the old railway zone system in Manchuria.

The foreign settlement system is closely bound up with the extra-territorial rights which the Western powers, beginning with Britain, acquired for their nationals by treaty. The Westerners in the ports were under the jurisdiction of their own consuls, lived in quarters of their own near their consulates and had their own police. In the long period of disorder and anti-foreign outbreaks in China they successfully asserted their claim to exclude Chinese police and soldiers from the settlements and to have their own armed forces—local volunteers or marines from their countries' warships. Originally suburban quarters, the settlements became in some cases—in particular at Shanghai and Tientsin—the principal business areas of their towns and drew in a Chinese population outnumbering the foreign residents. The growth of these autonomous un-national units— states within a state—provided a grave problem for the time when China should begin to organize a modern-style state administration, claiming in full the normal rights of sovereignty within her borders.

THE WESTERNERS

The patrolling of the Yangtse by foreign gunboats was instituted in connection with the foreign settlements up the river and the foreign-owned river shipping. The practice was a fertile source of incidents, the most notable of which was the battle fought by H.M.S. *Cockchafer* in 1926 with forces of the provincial army of Szechwan at Wanhsien more than a thousand miles from the sea.

The stationing of foreign detachments for the protection of the Legations in Peiping and the guarding of the railway to Tientsin was authorized by the treaty of 1901, which settled accounts for the "Boxer" anti-foreign outbreak of the previous year. The garrisons were meant to provide against renewed surprise attacks by anti-foreign bands, but, having once been established, they became a permanent institution, and the relevant clauses of the treaty have never yet been abrogated.

The railway zone system in Manchuria was introduced by the Russians, whose contract for the building of the Chinese Eastern Railway in 1896 gave the company (actually controlled by the Russian government) "absolute and exclusive right of administration of its lands" with its own police force. Owing to the prevalence of brigandage in Manchuria soldiers were brought in to serve as police, so that the railway became in effect a ribbon of Russian territory across Manchuria. The same rights were obtained by Russia in 1898 for the branch from Harbin to Port Arthur, a section of which was transferred to Japan in 1905 after the Russo-Japanese war and became the South Manchuria Railway; by the Treaty of Portsmouth the railway guards were limited to 15 per kilometer, but this was quite sufficient for a considerable force to be assembled anywhere along the line.

THE WESTERNERS

The semi-colonial servitudes on Chinese sovereignty were the result of China's failure to modernize her administrative and fiscal system during the second half of the nineteenth century. China retained enough strength and unity to survive as an independent state, but remained too weak and loosely organized either to give due protection to foreigners and their enterprises (which the official class in any case detested and had accepted only under *force majeure*) or to resist demands which were put to it on pretext of the disorderly conditions. The outcome of the long series of conflicts between the Western powers and the decaying Manchu-Chinese imperial regime was a compromise which made China a unique anomaly in international law, for, while continuing to hold rank as a sovereign state, she was deprived of the essential attributes of sovereignty inside her recognized frontiers. With foreign garrisons quartered in her territory and two alien-ruled municipalities in the heart of her biggest city, China was not, even after the Washington Conference of 1922, in possession of full sovereign rights. Chinese nationalism was inevitably imbued with a resolve to get rid of the "unequal treaties," but strong vested interests had come to be bound up with them, and the position was all the more difficult because certain of the privileges claimed by foreigners had long been conceded in practice without any real treaty basis.

Japan escaped from the servitudes imposed upon China by her rapid self-modernization after 1868. She was in the beginning subjected, like China, to a system of extra-territoriality, and in the period of her internal troubles in the sixties was widely expected to fall to pieces and be eaten up by Western imperialism much more easily than China. But, having equipped herself with an effectively centralized administration, a Western-model legal code and a competent army and navy, Japan avoided the regime of foreign garrisons and independent settlements, and secured the final abolition of extra-territoriality in 1901. Nor did she stop at her own emancipation; even before it was complete, she had joined the Western powers as a holder of extra-territorial rights on the mainland of Asia. The possession of such rights came to appear to the Japanese, from their own experience on the wrong side of it, to be the distinctive attribute of civilized states in relation to backward peoples, and its economic value was also appreciated. In Korea Japan was actually first in the field and secured a trade treaty with extra-territorial rights for her nationals in advance of any other nation. She obtained the same privileges in China by the Treaty of Shimonoseki after the Sino-Japanese war in 1895, and thus entered the ranks of the Western powers who already held them. Under the Boxer Protocol of 1901 she shared with the Western powers the right of keeping garrisons in the Peiping-Tientsin area. By the Treaty of Portsmouth in 1905 she took over part of the system of rights previously extorted by the Russians in Manchuria, including the Kwantung Leased Territory and the railway as far as Changchun with its privileges of administration and railway guards. In this way Japan gained a foothold inside China, and in the end the Western powers discovered that she was the principal beneficiary of a system they had originally elaborated for their own advantage.

Chapter IV

MANCHU EMPIRE AND CHINESE REPUBLIC

The Chinese empire, as constituted in the first decade of the present century, consisted of the eighteen provinces of China Proper and the four outer dependencies, Manchuria, Mongolia, Sinkiang or East Turkestan, and Tibet. China Proper comprised only 1,533,000 out of a total area of 4,278,000 square miles, but was estimated to contain well over 95 per cent of the total population.

This great empire was the creation of the Manchus, who captured Peking[1] in 1644 and set up the Ch'ing dynasty in China. The purely Chinese Ming dynasty, which had reigned from 1368 to 1644, had not held sway over northwest Manchuria, Mongolia, western Sinkiang or Tibet, though its territory in the time of its full vigor had extended northwestward by the Kansu corridor to Hami and northeastward to the lower Amur and the Japan Sea north of Korea. Toward the end of the Ming period the Chinese were confined within the Great Wall, while the Northland passed under the domination of two barbaric powers: the Kalmuks and the Manchus. The former, whose homeland was

[1] Now Peiping. Peking means "Northern Capital," and when it ceased to be the capital in 1928, its early name of Peiping was officially restored.

52

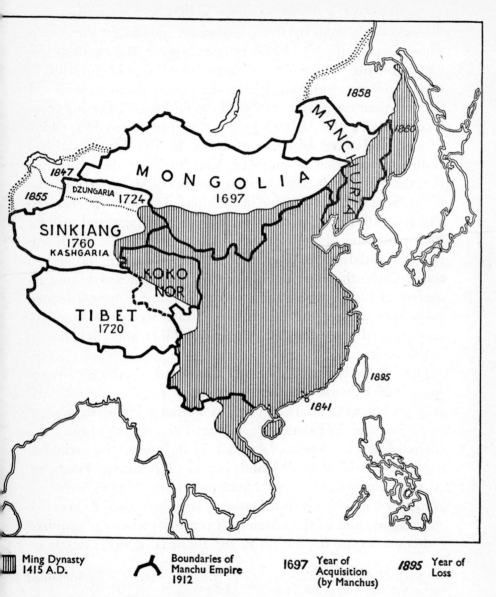

1858

1860

MANCHURIA

1847

MONGOLIA
1697

DZUNGARIA 1724

1855

SINKIANG
1760
KASHGARIA

KOKO
NOR

TIBET
1720

1895

1841

| | Ming Dynasty 1415 A.D. | | Boundaries of Manchu Empire 1912 | 1697 | Year of Acquisition (by Manchus) | 1895 | Year of Loss |

7. CHINA UNDER THE MING AND MANCHU DYNASTIES

in western Mongolia, were essentially nomadic; the latter, whose ascendancy was based on east-central Manchuria, combined shifting cultivation and horse-breeding with hunting in their economy, and were better able to amalgamate with the Chinese than the pure nomads. They conquered Liaoning province (Mukden and Dairen) before they penetrated into China Proper, and were affected culturally by the long-established Chinese population in southern Manchuria; at the same time they drew into their confederacy a number of Mongol tribes who aided them in their wars against China.[1] The Manchus entered China in 1644 to take part in a Chinese civil war and at once took possession of the capital (Peking), though the south was not fully subdued for a generation. Then, toward the end of the seventeenth century the Manchus, strengthened by the resources of China, where their power was now centered, turned their arms against the Kalmuks and in a series of campaigns incorporated the whole of Mongolia, Tibet and Sinkiang in their empire.

Outside the limits of Manchu-Chinese rule there were several states which could not be regarded as forming part of the empire, but were attached to it by formal acknowledgment of suzerainty and the payment of tribute. This category of countries included Korea, Luchu (Ryukyu in Japanese, the string of Japanese-inhabited small islands between Kyushu and Formosa), Annam, Burma and Nepal. Such relations of states were not recognized in Western international law based on the theory of sovereignty, and in the nineteenth century China was required either to accept responsibility for the acts of her "vassals"—

[1] Each of the Eight Banners (*pa ch'i*) of the Manchu army contained three sections—Manchu, Mongol and Chinese.

which she generally declined to do—or to disinterest herself in their fate. In the end Korea and Luchu were annexed by Japan, Annam by France, Burma by Britain, and Nepal, which retained a semi-independence inside the framework of British Indian paramountcy, ceased to pay tribute after the Chinese Revolution of 1911.

Within the internationally recognized borders of the Manchu empire the Manchu element gradually declined in importance and was swallowed up by the Chinese population. The state was always known to Europeans as "China" or the "Chinese empire," and Chinese was its official language.[1] The process of assimilation, moreover, was not limited to China Proper, but extended also, and in an even greater degree, to the Manchu homeland. The Manchu tribesmen, a warlike but never numerous community, were distributed in garrisons over the empire, and Manchuria itself was left almost empty; the Manchu emperors, wishing to preserve it as an exclusive domain of their race, at first prohibited the immigration of Chinese, but the prohibition was later on relaxed, and in the late nineteenth century Chinese settlement was positively encouraged in order to create a human barrier against the flow of Russian colonization east of Lake Baikal. Manchuria thus became almost purely Chinese, except for the arid western tracts which were left to Mongol nomads, and the Manchus virtually disappeared as a distinct nationality with a territory of their own; formally, however, the administration of Manchuria, "the three eastern provinces" (*tung san shêng*), was kept separate from that of China Proper, "the eighteen provinces" (*shih pa shêng*), until 1907.

---

[1] In the eighteenth century, however, official business between China and Russia was transacted in Manchu, and Manchu grammars and dictionaries were compiled by Russians.

MANCHU EMPIRE AND CHINESE REPUBLIC

The order established by the Manchu empire also led to an extension of Chinese settlement in two other regions beyond the Great Wall: Inner Mongolia and Sinkiang. In the former Chinese peasants encroached on cultivable steppe land at the expense of the Mongols' pastures, the government officials and Mongol princes finding profit for themselves in the process. In Sinkiang the settlement was more a matter of policy; colonies of Chinese and Manchus were planted, especially in the Kulja and Urumchi districts, to protect the western march of the empire, at first against the still unsubdued Kalmuks and later against Russia. In Tibet and Outer Mongolia, on the other hand, there was no Chinese colonization, and Chinese nationality was represented only by a handful of officials and traders.

Within China Proper there was evident throughout the period of the Manchu dynasty a deep cleavage between north and south in relation to the central government at Peking. In the words of a writer on Chinese history:[1] "The Manchus occupied northern China by consent, unopposed; they conquered the south by force after a long and bitter struggle. This fact dominated the later history of the dynasty, and still today explains the differing attitude of the northern and southern Chinese toward the Manchu dynasty and the imperial system."

The hostility of the south toward the Manchu regime was further accentuated by the penetration of Western cultural influences into the south in advance of their extension to the north, contacts with foreigners being made not only through the ports open to foreign trade—of which Shanghai was the most northerly from 1842 to 1858—but also through Chinese emigration, which came mainly from Kwantung to Malaya, the Dutch

[1] C. P. Fitzgerald, *China: a Short Cultural History*, p. 535.

East Indies and America. The great T'ai P'ing rebellion, which broke out in 1851, was not only anti-Manchu, but also Christian; it began in Kwangsi, and its advance, first to Hankow and then down the Yangtse to Nanking, foreshadowed the later progress of the Kuomintang forces from Canton to the North China Plain. The T'ai P'ing rebellion was finally suppressed in 1864, but the cleavage between north and south was not overcome, and Canton subsequently became the focus of the revolutionary, modernizing, nationalist movement in China.[1]

The T'ai P'ing rebels sought to supplant the Manchu dynasty, not to break up the unity of the empire; the Moslem rebellions which occurred during the same period threatened, however, the disruption of Chinese sovereignty. Independent kingdoms, which made appeals for British protection, were set up in Sinkiang and Yunnan, and the Russians took the opportunity to occupy Kulja and the Ili basin in 1871. But the Chinese in the end crushed the Moslem revolts and recovered Kulja by negotiation. The empire within the frontiers of 1860 was thus preserved intact until the Sino-Japanese war of 1894 brought Chinese sovereignty in Manchuria into peril.

The war was fought on the issue of Chinese suzerainty over Korea, but military operations were also carried into southern Manchuria, and by the Treaty of Shimonoseki the Liaotung peninsula, including Port Arthur, was ceded to Japan. Russia, however, persuaded France and Germany to join her in compelling Japan by an ultimatum to restore this territory to China, and then took advantage of her position as China's protector to penetrate Manchuria herself. In 1898 she compelled China to

[1] The Cantonese did not support the T'ai P'ing movement, whose leader belonged to the distinct Hakka community of Kwangtung Chinese.

grant her a lease of Port Arthur, which she proceeded to turn into a fortress and naval base; this stronghold together with the Russian-controlled railways gave the Russians paramount influence in Manchuria, and when in 1900 the Boxer anti-foreign outbreak was made the excuse for a general military occupation, the country passed completely under Russian dominion. The Russian rule was not destined to last long, for in 1904 Japan, covered against French or German intervention by the Anglo-Japanese alliance, made war on Russia and expelled her forces from Port Arthur and Mukden. This did not, however, result in a full restoration of Chinese sovereign control in Manchuria, for, though the Treaty of Portsmouth required a withdrawal of all troops, Russian or Japanese, outside the Kwantung Leased Territory (Port Arthur) and the railway zones, these corridors of foreign power remained, only they were now shared between Russia and Japan. Nor could China count after 1907 on the mutual hostility of Russia and Japan, for, having fought each other, they soon entered into close political collaboration, and by private arrangement between themselves partitioned all Chinese territory north of the Great Wall into "spheres of influence"—Russia to have North Manchuria, Outer Mongolia and Sinkiang, while Japan reserved to herself South Manchuria and Inner Mongolia.

The Russian empire-building in Manchuria from 1896 to 1904 was supplemented by Russian intrigues in Tibet, which brought about British intervention and a military expedition to Lhasa in 1904, Chinese control of Tibet being at that time very slight. To reassert the authority of Peking a Chinese army was sent to Tibet in 1908 and had just succeeded in its task when the Chinese Revolution broke out in 1911.

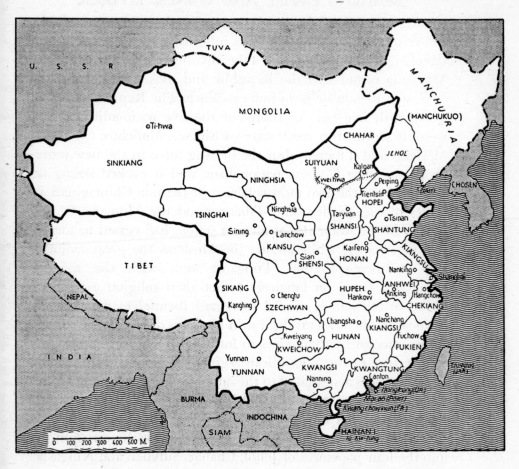

8. PROVINCES OF CHINA IN THE LAST TEN YEARS

MANCHU EMPIRE AND CHINESE REPUBLIC

After the fall of the Manchu dynasty the Chinese Republic was recognized internationally as inheriting all the territories of the old empire, but both the Tibetans and the Mongols of Outer Mongolia repudiated the Republic and took advantage of the confusion to gain *de facto* independence. The Republic adopted a flag with five bars to represent the five nationalities which were to form the new state—Chinese, Manchus, Mongols, Moslems and Tibetans, but the driving force in the new movement was pure Chinese nationalism, and it evoked strong resistance from the two most coherent of the non-Chinese nationalities of the empire—the Tibetans and the Mongols. Of the other two the Manchus, as already stated, had ceased to form a real nationality, while among the Moslems the great majority were Chinese-speaking (Tungans) and, with the modern nationalist stress on language rather than religion as the criterion of allegiance, tended to regard themselves primarily as Chinese in the new era; the Turki Moslems of Sinkiang were not strong enough by themselves to form an independent state.

A feature of the Republican regime has been the creation of new provinces assimilated to the administrative system of China Proper in those nearer parts of Tibet and Mongolia which remained under Chinese control. Sikang and Tsinghai were carved out of eastern Tibet, while Inner Mongolia was split up into the four provinces of Jehol, Chahar, Suiyüan and Ninghsia.

Apart from the Tibetan and Mongol secessions, however, there was a great disintegration of the Chinese state after 1915. The military governors of provinces engrossed the provincial revenues and made war on one another with private armies in the manner of feudal barons. Their insubordination was supported to some extent by the traditional particularism of

Chinese provinces and their reluctance to submit to a centralized fiscal system, but in no case was there a real separatist
movement aimed at setting up a new sovereign state. Among
educated Chinese the consciousness of nationality was continually growing stronger, and the Kuomintang party with its headquarters at Canton was building up a powerful nationalist
movement with a program of "rights recovery," "abolition of
unequal treaties," state unification and economic self-develop-
ment. Nevertheless, as long as the regional *tuchün* despotisms
and civil wars continued, China was even weaker in relation to
foreign powers than she had been under the Manchus, and her
economic evolution was held up; the country's substance was
devoured by unproductive spoliation and brigandage, and
foreign capital did not dare to venture in under conditions of
such disorder except where it was assured of political control.

At the Washington Conference in 1922 eight nations agreed
with China in the so-called Nine-Power Treaty to "provide the
fullest and most unembarrassed opportunity to China to develop
and maintain for herself an effective and stable government."
Such a prospect corresponded on the whole to the policies of
Britain and the U.S.A., who took the lead at the Conference;
a third signatory, however, was by no means of one mind with
regard to the desirability of assisting the growth of a strong,
united China. Influential official and business circles in Japan
believed that their country had a vested interest in Chinese dis-
union, and that the unification and industrialization of China
would spell Japan's political and economic decline. In particular
they feared that a nationalist Chinese central government controlling Manchuria would soon make an end of the existing
monopoly position of the South Manchuria Railway.

Chapter V

THE EXPANSION OF JAPAN

In 1853, when Commodore Perry demanded the opening of Japan to foreign trade, Japan was almost completely secluded from the outer world and her dominion was confined to the four large islands from Kyushu to Yezo (Hokkaido).[1] She had no foothold on the mainland of Asia. To the southwest of Kyushu, the Ryukyu islands, which are now an integral part of Japan, then formed a separate kingdom which paid tribute to China, though also recognizing a certain suzerainty of the Japanese lords of Satsuma in Kyushu. To the north of Yezo Japanese fishermen and petty traders frequented the shores of Sakhalin and the Kurile islands, but there was no Japanese administration. Yezo itself was scarcely Japanese except in the extreme south; most of it was wild forest country still left to the primitive Aino aborigines. Japan in effect consisted of Honshu, Shikoku, Kyushu and the closely adjacent small islands.

Under the seclusionist system established early in the seventeenth century Japanese subjects were not allowed to go abroad, for trade or any other purpose, on pain of death if they returned; foreigners were not allowed in Japan except for a very limited

[1] Hokkaido is really the name for an administrative division including Yezo and the Kuriles, but it has come to be used as a synonym for Yezo by itself.

trade, open only to the Chinese and Dutch, in the port of Nagasaki. From 1615 to 1853 Japan had no foreign war and no serious internal revolt; this period affords the most striking contrast to the stormy history of modern Japan.

Since prehistoric times (before A.D. 200) Japan has never been successfully invaded. The attempts made by Kublai Khan, the Mongol emperor of China, in the thirteenth century resulted in complete disaster, and the failure of what was then the strongest power in Asia to subdue the islands of the "Yamato race" gave the Japanese a traditional confidence in the divinely assured inviolability of their country. The Kublai Khan invasion has the same place in Japanese, as the Spanish Armada in English, memory; the inscription "He blew with His winds and they were scattered" on the pedestal of Drake's monument at Plymouth affords an exact counterpart to "the divine wind of Ise," the typhoon which wrecked the fleet of China's overlord. This tradition of security goes far to explain the remarkable vigor of the national awakening when the Japanese in the eighteen-fifties suddenly found their coasts and ports at the mercy of foreign warships.

Prior to the Sino-Japanese war of 1894 the Japanese had twice in their history made temporary conquests on the Asiatic mainland. At an uncertain date some time before A.D. 400 they penetrated into Korea, that country being at the time divided into several small kingdoms; in 663 they were finally expelled by an alliance of the Korean kingdom of Shinra with China, and Korea was united by Shinra under Chinese suzerainty. From 663 to 1592 there was no Japanese intervention in continental affairs, though the coasts of Kyushu were a base for corsairs who sorely harried the peoples of the mainland; then the great soldier

THE EXPANSION OF JAPAN

Hideyoshi, having united Japan under his own rule (formally subject to the authority of the Mikado) after a long period of civil wars, designed the conquest of China and invaded Korea as a preliminary. After a campaign of varying fortunes the troops were withdrawn on the death of Hideyoshi in 1598, and the war came to be known as the *Ryo-to Fa-bi* or "Dragon's head and snake's tail" because of its glorious beginning and inglorious ending. From 1598 no further attempt at continental expansion was made until after the "westernization" of Japan.

With the entry of Japan into a world of international relations and modern navies the possession of outlying islands came to be of great importance, and it was to these that Japan's attention was first directed after the "Restoration" of 1868. In 1875 a treaty was made with Russia whereby Russia acquired sovereignty over Sakhalin and Japan over the Kuriles (Chishima). The Bonin islands (Ogasawarajima) to the southeast of Japan were formally annexed in 1876, and the Ryukyu islands (with a Japanese-speaking population) in 1879, China's claim to suzerainty over the latter being ignored.[1] The Kuriles, the Bonins and Ryukyu were incorporated in the administrative system of Japan Proper and are not today counted as colonial territories.

The acquisition of a definitely colonial domain began with the annexation of Taiwan (Formosa), which was ceded by China after the war of 1894-5. The Liaotung peninsula of southern Manchuria, which had been occupied by the Japanese army during the war, was also ceded by the same peace treaty, but was restored to China after the ultimatum known as the Triple Intervention, in which Russia, France and Germany partici-

[1] The former king of Ryukyu was given a title in the Japanese peerage.

9. THE TERRITORIAL EXPANSION OF JAPAN

pated. During the next few years it seemed likely that Russia would swallow up both Manchuria and Korea and exclude Japan from any possibility of expansion on the mainland, but the Russo-Japanese war of 1904-5 turned the tables and left Japanese forces in control of Korea, southern Manchuria and most of the island of Sakhalin. By the Treaty of Portsmouth, which concluded the war, Russia ceded to Japan half of Sakhalin and the leasehold of Port Arthur and Dalny (Kwantung), which she had acquired from China; Korea, nominally a sovereign state since 1895, was placed under a thinly disguised Japanese protectorate and was finally annexed in 1910. At the time of the outbreak of the Great War in 1914 Japan thus held four colonial territories: Taiwan, Chosen (Korea), Karafuto (southern Sakhalin) and Kwantung, and as a result of the Great War she obtained a fifth—the island groups in the Pacific north of the Equator which had belonged to Germany. Of the five, three— Taiwan, Chosen and Karafuto—were under Japan's full sovereignty; in the other two her sovereignty was qualified, Kwantung being held on lease from China, and the ex-German islands under a mandate of the League of Nations.

The conquests made by Japanese armies in Manchuria, Mongolia and China since 1931 have effected no formal addition to the Japanese empire, for a method of "indirect rule" has been applied without any annexation or even protectorate of the ordinary kind; Manchukuo is in Japanese theory a sovereign state, and any nation which so desires can have diplomatic representation at Hsinking—at the price of recognizing Manchukuo's sovereignty and detachment from China. The world in general does not take this theory very seriously and regards Manchukuo as merely an alias for Japan. But in keeping up the elaborate hocus-pocus of independence for a country she in reality controls Japan is simply following an example set by Britain with the concurrence of the League of Nations, for the admission of India in 1919 to a society whose membership is by its constitution restricted to independent states and "fully self-governing" colonies or dominions introduced into international relations an element of sheer humbug which the world will yet have cause to regret. If a state can be recognized as "fully self-governing" when it lacks every attribute of real independence, the way is open for an unlimited faking of sovereignty. By virtue of the Geneva conception of national independence Japan can at least claim that the people of Manchuria have not enjoyed less freedom in setting up the government of Manchukuo than has the "fully self-governing" Indian nation in choosing Lord Linlithgow as its ruler.

In effect the Japanese empire at the time of writing extends to Paotou on the Yellow River and Kiukiang on the Yangtse, and its limits are the fronts of the Japanese armies in the field. The populations under Japanese rule outside Japan already outnumber the conquering nation, whereas up to 1931 the inhabitants of the colonies were in a ratio of only about 3:7 to those of the homeland.

Japan Proper has an area of 147,611 square miles (slightly larger than Great Britain, but smaller than any one of thirteen out of the eighteen provinces of China Proper) and a population of over 70 million. The Japanese in their islands form a very well-defined and compact nationality, and except for the negligible remnant of the Aino aborigines in Hokkaido (now only 20,000 strong) Japan has no domestic nationality problem. It should be remembered, however, in relation to internal politics that, although Japan is a small country inhabited by a single nationality, its surface is so much intersected by mountains as well as by the insular divisions that a very strong local particularism prevails, and "county town" influences are an effective counterweight to the political activity of the big cities. London is not Britain and Paris is not France; it is even more true that Tokyo is not Japan, in spite of a centralized unitary system of administration. Up to seventy years ago Japan was divided into small feudal units, many of which were very loosely attached to the central power, and the old loyalties persist, so that Japanese opinion is formed no less in such places as Kagoshima, Saga and Kanazawa than in the capital, and the cliques in national politics often have narrowly local roots. The strong district attachments provide a framework for the separate life of rural Japan, industry being concentrated in a few restricted areas in the southeast of Honshu and the extreme north of Kyushu. The army in Japan specially represents the countryside, for most of the officers come from the small landowning gentry and the conscripts are selected as far as possible from peasant stock rather than from the town population.

The directly ruled colonies have a total population of about 30 million, of which less than 2 million are Japanese, the remainder being made up of about 22 million Koreans, 6 million Chinese in Formosa and Kwantung, and one to two hundred thousand Formosa aborigines and natives of the Mandated Islands. To this total must now be added, as for the time being subject to Japan, over 30 millions in Manchukuo and approximately 100 millions (minus refugees) in the areas occupied by Japan in China Proper since the outbreak of hostilities last year; all these are Chinese except for some

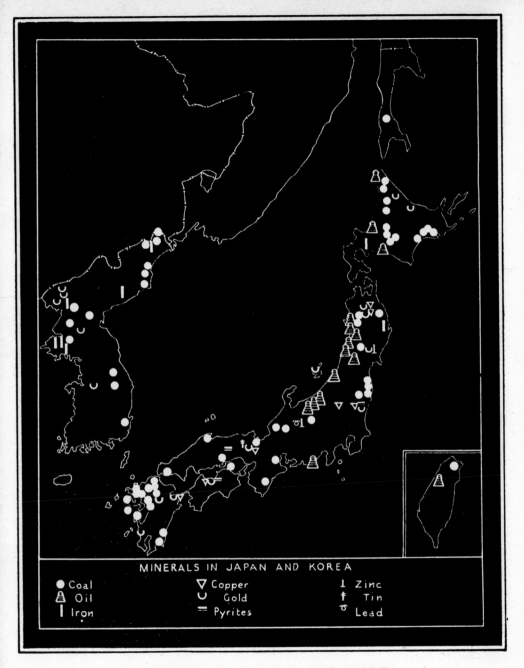

10. MINERALS IN JAPAN AND KOREA

three million Mongols in the west of Manchukuo and in Inner Mongolia.

The history of Japan's expansion falls into two periods corresponding to the distinction between her formal and her informal empire. The colonial territories acquired up to 1931 were all of some value, but they did not give Japan in the long run a strong economic position either for commercial competition in a world of increasing economic nationalism or for war-power under conditions of strategy in which military decision was tending more and more to depend on capacity for avoiding economic breakdown in time of war. Japan and Korea were more or less self-sufficing as regards foodstuffs, and Formosa on the edge of the tropics supplemented their resources with sugar, citrus fruits and other special products. In minerals, however, and in the raw materials of several of her most important industries Japan remained largely or entirely dependent on imports for essential supplies. Japan is not rich in any important mineral except copper; her resources of coal are small, of iron ore insignificant, and of oil negligible, for a country which aims at large-scale industrial development. Good coking coal is conspicuous by its absence. For textile industries cotton must be entirely, and wool almost entirely, imported; the rayon industry is also partly dependent on wood-pulp imports.

To create big industries and support a large population by the export of manufactured goods with so inadequate a basis of natural resources would be a formidable task even in a world of free trade, stable currencies and general political harmony. Under the conditions prevailing in the world since 1919, and still more since 1930, industrialization has involved Japan in very serious difficulties, and the most disconcerting factor in the

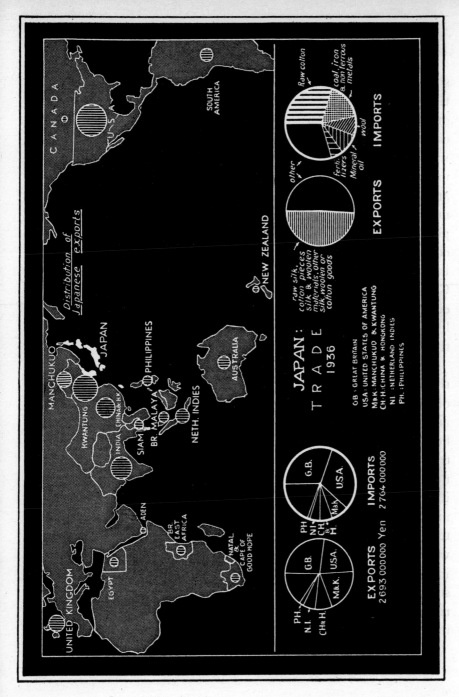

II. JAPANESE TRADE 1936

situation has been the prospect of the competitive industrialization of China. For China not only has five times the population of Japan, but is far better endowed with natural resources and capacity for raw-material production, especially as regards coal, iron and cotton. If China and Japan had begun their self-modernization simultaneously about 1870 and had continued at the same rate, there can be no doubt but that China would now be the Great Power of the Far East, both economically and politically, and that Japan would still be a mainly agricultural country and a power of secondary rank, comparing with China in much the same way as Holland or Sweden with Britain or Germany. But China's late start gave Japan a long lead both in economic development and military power, and to retain this lead has been the main preoccupation of Japanese policy for the last decade.

If a united and efficiently administered China were to carry through a program of industrialization with her advantages of abundant cheap labor equal to Japan's and with superior natural resources, she would quickly surpass Japan both in heavy and light industries, competing ruinously with Japanese trade both in the Chinese home market (covered by tariffs if necessary) and elsewhere, and also reducing Japan to inferiority in power by a greater and more self-sufficient capacity for war-material production. Even if Japan were prepared to contemplate such an economic and political abdication, adjustment would be extremely difficult with a momentum of population increase adapted to an expanding economic system, and the strain on the social structure would probably lead to domestic revolution. Hence the "positive" policy toward China, which means, in short, to keep China weak and divided, to prevent a

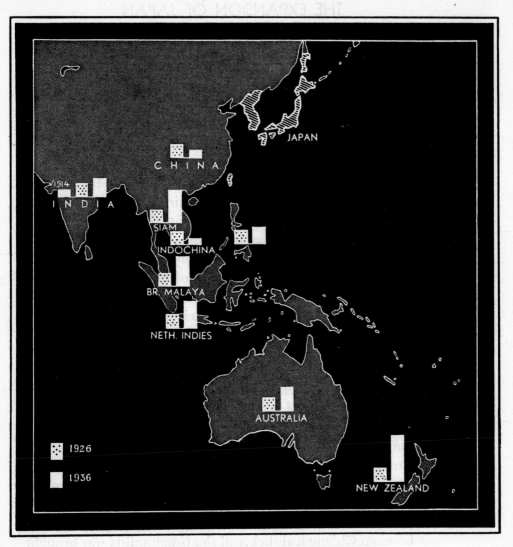

JAPAN

CHINA

1914
INDIA

SIAM

INDOCHINA

BR. MALAYA

NETH. INDIES

AUSTRALIA

1926

1936

NEW ZEALAND

12. JAPANESE TRADE EXPANSION

Kuomintang-directed, anti-Japanese industrialization of China, and to control the raw material resources of the country for Japan's own use in peace or war.

Japanese liberals during the nineteen-twenties believed that a satisfactory compromise was possible, and they might have reached an understanding with the new China but for the fundamental conflict over Japan's vested interests in South Manchuria —interests which were based on the political supremacy taken over from Russia in 1905 and were regarded by Chinese nationalists as incompatible with China's sovereignty. The conflict reached a climax in 1931, at a time when Japan was in the throes of a serious internal crisis due to the effects of a world-wide economic depression, and the army chiefs took the opportunity to launch Japan on a new era of imperialist expansion. The military occupation of Manchuria not only secured the vested interests of the South Manchuria Railway but delivered all the resources of four Chinese provinces into the hands of Japan. Some Japanese leaders hoped to close the account with the completion of this conquest. There could, however, be no stopping at the borders of Manchuria. China now became implacably hostile and acquired a new political unity and energy from the principle of "anti-Japanism"; her capacity for economic development was not seriously impaired by the loss of Manchuria, for her most important economic areas lay south of the Great Wall. In 1935 China reformed her currency with British financial support and advice, and at the beginning of 1937, as a result of the Sian kidnaping incident, the civil war between Chiang Kai-shek and the Communists was brought to an end and replaced by an anti-Japanese People's Front. Meanwhile the tariff and quota restrictions on Japanese export trade and exchange difficulties due to inflationary finance had combined to convert Japanese business circles to a program of obtaining economic control over the raw-material resources of North China; the fighting services favored the same policy as a means of both forestalling the growth of China's war-power and strengthening their own. In these circumstances, after four years of uneasy truce, the war against China was renewed at the end of July 1937.

75

Chapter VI

SOVIET SIBERIA

The territories of the Soviet Union stretch to the northwest, north and northeast of both China and Japan—Petropavlovsk in Kamchatka is nearly 20 degrees of longitude east of Tokyo—and in Far Eastern politics the Russian power established between Lake Baikal and the Pacific stands at the apex of the triangle of which China and Japan form the base. The obvious strategic importance of East Siberia, however, and its vast size on the map do not at all correspond to its significance in the economy of the Soviet Union. It is by far the poorest both actually and potentially (on known data) of the main regions of the Union, and if all territory east of the Yenisei were to be eliminated tomorrow, the Soviet economic system would hardly be affected by the loss, except perhaps as regards gold-mining and the fur trade.

The economic power of the Soviet Union and its future prospects in world affairs are based on its enormous natural resources in soil and minerals. The great belt of *chernozyom* or "black earth" soil from the Dniester to the Yenisei provides the possibility of an abundant agricultural production, while enormous reserves of coal and iron ore in European Russia and West Siberia afford an adequate foundation for a heavy industry on the largest scale. Add to these assets the oil of the Caucasus, the copper and cotton of Turkestan, the timber of the north, the broad cattle and sheep pastures of the steppe margins and the fact that Russia is all plain, except for the Urals, from the Baltic to the Altai, and the whole of that area is seen to form a grand economic unit of prodigious natural wealth. But East Siberia falls outside that area and forms a separate region in no way comparable in natural resources. It has virtually no black-earth soil and very little cultivable land; it is in great part as mountainous as it is barren; except for gold, deposits of which are found mainly in the Lena basin, it has no mineral wealth remotely comparable to that of European Russia or West Siberia; communications are inadequate for such resources as there are and can only be developed at great expense.[1] The principal maritime outlet, Vladivostok, does not find a place in the first rank of Far Eastern ports in respect of tonnage cleared. In a process of normal economic development East Siberia would remain a region of "bad lands" like northern Canada, productive of gold and furs with a supplement of lumber and fisheries, but a mere appendage to the main economy of the Soviet Union. Its recent development, under the direction of central government planning, has been highly artificial and dominated by strategic-political considerations, which require the existence of an agricultural and coal-metal base to support Soviet military power in the Far East.

In 1931 the population of East Siberia, including considerable territory to the west of the Yenisei, was as follows:

Far Eastern Region (of R.S.F.S.R.) . . . 1,593,400
Yakutsk Republic 308,400

[1] Gold and furs from Yakutia are at present transported mainly by air.

SOVIET SIBERIA

Buryat-Mongol Republic	575,000
East Siberian Region (of R.S.F.S.R.) . .	2,568,400
Total .	5,045,200

A population of rather over 5 millions in this vast area—and it has not greatly increased since 1931—is little enough in comparison with over 400 millions in China and nearly 100 millions in Japan and Korea. Moreover, it has not been attained without great efforts to promote colonization, begun by the Tsarist government after the Russo-Japanese war, when the emptiness of East Siberia was revealed as a great handicap to the Russian army operating in Manchuria. Soviet policy has sought to induce settlers to come east of Lake Baikal—and stay there—by drastic exemptions from taxation; another device has been the founding of the autonomous area of Biro-Bijan as a colony for Jews in the country north of the Amur. Labor for road and railway construction has been supplied in recent years by convicts, who were available in large quantities after the liquidation of the kulaks under the First Five-Year Plan. By special inducements to some and coercion for others the Soviet government has during the last decade assembled in East Siberia a greater number of Russians than would otherwise have gone there, but the total effect on the wilderness has not been very great, and the Soviet Far Eastern army still relies less on local agriculture and industries than on its magazines and its railway communications with the west.

The Trans-Siberian railway has lately been double-tracked and this has vastly increased its efficiency as a route of supply. Now that the Manchurian section of the direct Chita-Vladivostok line (the old Chinese Eastern Railway) has been sold to

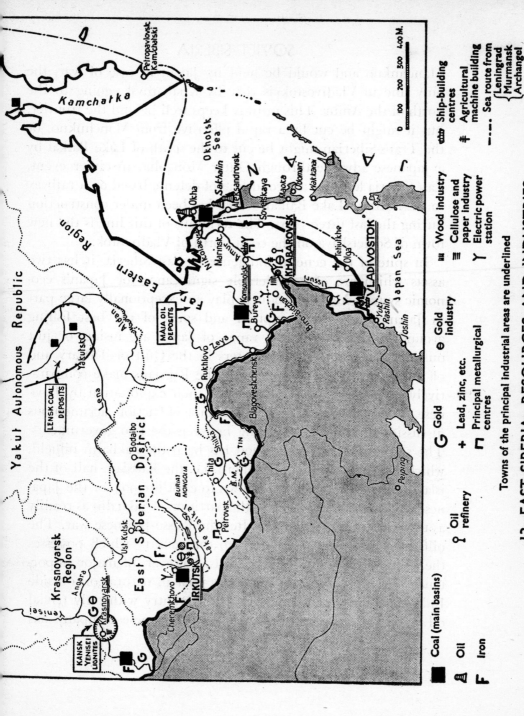

13. EAST SIBERIA: RESOURCES AND INDUSTRIES

Towns of the principal industrial areas are underlined

■ Coal (main basins)
♨ Oil
F Iron

G Gold
♀ Oil refinery

⊖ Gold industry
+ Lead, zinc, etc.
∏ Principal metallurgical centres

⚒ Ship-building centres
⚵ Agricultural machine building

Ⅲ Wood industry
≣ Cellulose and paper industry
Y Electric power station

---- Sea route from Leningrad Murmansk Archangel

0 100 200 300 400 M.

Manchukuo and would be held by Japan in case of war, the only line to Vladivostok is that by Khabarovsk, going to the north of the Amur. This railway keeps well behind the frontier, but it might be cut by a rapid offensive from Manchukuo, or the Trans-Siberian might be cut to the south of Lake Baikal by a Japanese advance through Outer Mongolia; in either event, East Siberia has now a second line of defense based on a railway to the north of Lake Baikal, which has been under construction during the last three years. The terminus of this line is the new town of Sovietskaya on the coast north of Vladivostok.

In spite of the general indigence of East Siberia, it has two assets which are of considerable significance for Japan's economic system. Marine products play an exceptionally large part in Japanese food consumption and some of the best fishing grounds within convenient range of Japan are inside, or just outside, Russian territorial waters in the Gulf of Tartary and off the west coast of Kamchatka. The Russians make comparatively little use of these fisheries and their exploitation by Japanese fishing fleets has long been a source of friction, acrimonious discussion and hard bargaining between the two governments. The second bone of contention has been the Sakhalin oilfield, which lies entirely in the northern, i.e. the Russian, half of the island. The oilfield was not known to exist in 1905, or the Japanese would not have agreed to the partition of Sakhalin as readily as they did in the settlement after the Russo-Japanese war. The oilfield is of little consequence to the country which possesses the wells of Baku and Grozni; it is, however, of major importance to the Far East, which is very poor in natural oil outside Indonesia, and especially to Japan, a country with only trivial oil resources of its own. Since 1925 a Japanese company has

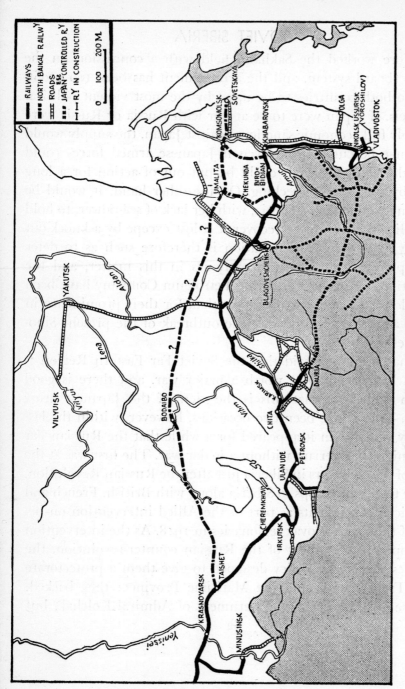

14. EAST SIBERIA: COMMUNICATIONS

therefore worked the Sakhalin field with a concession on the checkerboard system, and the arrangement has been too profitable to both countries to be upset by the most violent political quarrels. If Japan were to be at war with Russia or Russia were to apply full economic sanctions against Japan, the supply would of course be cut off, and even if Japanese armed forces could seize the field, the wells could be put out of action for a long time by competent wrecking. On the other hand, it would be extremely difficult for Russia, with her lack of sea-power, to hold Sakhalin in a war, or to recover it if lost except by a knock-out victory elsewhere. The situation is therefore such as to deter both powers from going to extremes in this matter, and the operations of the Kita Karafuto Petroleum Company have been notable for their obscurity rather than for their prominence in world affairs, especially since the outbreak of the present Sino-Japanese war.

It has been well said that the Soviet Far Eastern Region is worth having, but not worth a major war, and there is good reason to believe that this is the view of the Japanese army chiefs. There have been two occasions, however, within the last twenty years when it appeared for a while that the Russian Far East might be overrun without a major war. The first was at the time of the civil wars in Siberia just after the Russian Revolution. Japan then sent troops to Siberia along with British, French and American contingents as part of the Allied intervention on behalf of the Czechoslovak legionaries in 1918. As the intervention developed into support of the Russian counter-revolution, the Japanese evolved a policy designed to give them a protectorate over Transbaikalia and the Maritime Province; they backed, not the would-be central government of Admiral Kolchak, but the Cossack adventurers Semenov and Kalmikov who fought, each for his own hand, in East Siberia. The project failed, partly because of the solidarity of Russian national feeling against the Japanese and their protégés, partly because the Japanese military forces at that time lacked sufficient warm clothing to enable them to remain in the field during the Siberian winter in more than fifty degrees of frost. There was a lack of enthusiasm for the campaign in Japan, and the U.S.A. applied pressure for withdrawal. Finally, the Japanese evacuated Vladivostok in the autumn of 1922; they stayed in the Russian half of Sakhalin until 1925, and secured the oilfield concession already mentioned in consideration of their departure.

When the Russians started to develop Vladivostok as an air base, Japanese army leaders began to think the place had been too lightly given up, and another opportunity to lay hold on the Maritime Province seemed to offer itself in 1932. When the Kwantung Army took the offensive in southern Manchuria in September 1931, the Soviet Union was just entering on the critical period of the First Five-Year Plan and was incapable of any vigorous action externally; the Japanese, therefore, in confidence of immunity from Russian intervention in Manchuria, followed up their initial drive in their own railway sphere with an advance across the zone of the Russian-controlled Chinese Eastern Railway and up to the Amur. They thus placed themselves astride the principal line of communication with Vladivostok, and a policy group in the army advocated the seizure of all Soviet territory south of the Amur by a rapid offensive while the going was good. However, the fighting which broke out at Shanghai early in 1932 not only diverted Japan's attention elsewhere, but brought her into a position of such diplomatic isolation that a further military adventure was out of the question. The military party therefore contented itself with the elimination of Soviet interests and influence from Manchuria, which was a solid achievement and greatly strengthened Japan's strategic position.

Since 1933 Russia's defensive strength in the Far East has been so much increased that an invasion of Siberia or surprise attack on Vladivostok has not been a practical proposition for Japan. Nevertheless there has been a state of high tension between Japan and Russia, and a succession of lively border incidents has fed the rumor of an impending war. The Communists have made it almost an article of faith that Japanese penetration of China is merely preparation for an attack on the Soviet Union. But for an economically motivated imperialism there is no sense in seeking to acquire a territory that is at once poverty-stricken and strongly defended when richer and weaker lands lie close within reach. The anti-Soviet agitation in the Japanese army appears to be due partly to ideological and partly to strategic considerations, and it also has a distinct value to the military party in its psychological effect on the Japanese public.

However far the Soviet state under Stalin may have departed from the principles of Lenin and the Old Bolsheviks, it continues to stand for republicanism, anti-feudalism and agrarian revolution, and is therefore anathema to the social class which the Japanese officers' corps mainly represents. In China Communism has compromised with landlords, but only in order to unite the Chinese nation in the cause of anti-Japanism. On all counts the Japanese emperor-revering, feudally minded "double patriot" fears and detests communist Russia. But such a sentiment, though it is an important political factor, is not likely to drive

84

Japan into war with Russia unless it coincides with the economic urge of Japanese expansion, and this urge is otherwise directed. There is even a group of business interests which advocates an understanding with the Soviet Union in order that Japan may concentrate on an anti-British policy; this group is not dominant, but its mere existence is very significant.

Strategically the Japanese military attitude is determined by fear of Russian intervention on behalf of China. The building of strategic railways and display of military strength toward the Soviet border are deterrent by intention; these measures are essentially defensive as regards Russia, though their purpose is to cover offensive strategy in China. Since the middle of last year some 400,000 Japanese troops have been held in Manchukuo to guard against any Russian move to render direct military aid to China, and though actual war has so far been avoided, the need for such a concentration has made the struggle with China far more difficult and costly than it would otherwise have been. Japan has had to fight in China with one arm while keeping the northern gate firmly shut with the other.

The strength of the Soviet Far Eastern army and the menace of the bombers at Vladivostok to the cities of Japan are genuine preoccupations of the Japanese General Staff. But the danger involves a compensating advantage, which would make a *rapprochement* with Russia something of a disaster for the military party. It is not possible to obtain strong popular support for an expansionist policy involving heavy sacrifices unless the people have a sense of being themselves threatened. The Vladivostok bombers are a threat to Japan's power, but they are an asset to Japanese militarism just because they put the country in danger. By frequent air-raid drills carried out with great realism in the larger cities the Japanese man-in-the-street is made conscious of the devastation that may come at any time from the other side of the Japan Sea and is more reconciled to the taxation he has to pay for the nation's swollen armaments and continental wars.

If war were to break out between Japan and Russia, there is no doubt but that Russian bombers from coastal bases on the Japan Sea could do serious damage in Japan. The distance from Vladivostok to Tsuruga is 490 miles (as compared with 386 miles, Hamburg to Hull) and Kyoto and Osaka are only a little farther on. Tokyo is less exposed, because bombers would have to fly over the mountains of Shinano or Kotsuke, where anti-aircraft batteries at high altitudes might be very troublesome. The vital centers of Japan are certainly vulnerable to air attack, whereas those of Russia are out of reach for Japan; on the other hand, it seems unlikely that the war could be decided by air action alone, and on the ground the remoteness of the real bases of Russian power would tell in favor of Japan in a struggle in which the Japanese stood on the defensive, especially if they were to evacuate the Amur salient and concentrate on holding Harbin with the Gobi desert covering Jehol and Chahar. Unless it were quickly decided by some remarkable military victory or by an internal convulsion in Japan, it appears probable that the emptiness and vast distances of East Siberia and Mongolia would make such a war more exhausting for Russia than for her enemy.

Chapter VII

MANCHUKUO

The territory of the state of Manchukuo, created by the agency of Japanese military power in 1932, comprises the former Chinese provinces of Liaoning, Kirin, Heilungkiang and Jehol. The first three of these were known to the Chinese as "the Three Eastern Provinces" and made up the area known to foreigners as Manchuria; Jehol was reckoned a part of Inner Mongolia. All four, however, prior to the Japanese conquest were under the control of the military despotism established in the years following the Chinese revolution by the adventurer Chang Tso-lin and inherited in 1928 by his son Chang Hsüeh-liang.

Manchuria is geographically separated from China Proper by the inner gulf of the Yellow Sea and by the mountains which shut in the North China plain and extend to the coast at Shanhaikwan. The Great Wall follows the line of these mountains and was designed to keep the passes by which barbarian raiders from Manchuria and Mongolia broke into the lowlands of Hopei; it never formed, however, an absolute limit to Chinese settlement, and for the last two thousand years the northern shore of the Yellow Sea with the hinterland as far as Mukden has been inhabited by Chinese. The northern and central parts of Manchuria, on the other hand, remained up to the nineteenth

87

century in the hands of primitive tribes of Mongol or Tungusic speech; sometimes a strong Chinese dynasty would reduce them to subjection, but more often the tribes would form a conquering confederacy or kingdom and bring the Chinese pale under their yoke. Manchuria was thus a country which always contained a strong Chinese element, but still remained a "frontier" and never became part of the Chinese homeland until quite recently.

To the west Manchuria merges into Mongolia without any very clear definition. The Great Khingan mountains, forming the eastern escarpment of the Mongolian plateau, are to some extent a dividing line, but the Barga district of Heilungkiang lies to the west of the range, while the arid steppe country typical of Mongolia is continued in a large tract to the east of it. Ethnically also the Mongols overflow to the east of the Great Khingan. Broadly speaking, however, there is a strong contrast between the two regions, in that most of Manchuria is arable and well provided with rivers, whereas most of Mongolia is riverless and too arid for cultivation.

It has already been pointed out (Chap. IV) that, as an ultimate result of the Manchu conquest of China, Manchuria became more Chinese than ever before; that the country fell virtually under Russian rule from 1900 to 1904; and that Chinese sovereignty was only imperfectly restored after the Russo-Japanese war. The seeds which came to harvest in 1931 were sown by the Treaty of Portsmouth in 1905. Manchuria was recognized as Chinese territory under Chinese administration, but the Russian railway system with its military guards and its "absolute and exclusive administration of its lands" remained, only it was now shared between Russia and Japan.

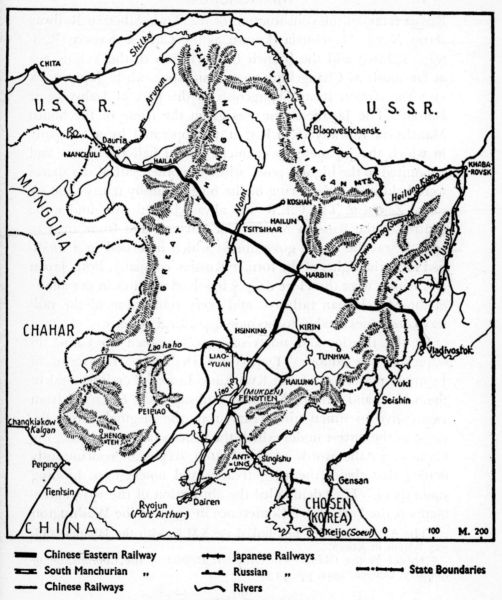

15. MANCHURIAN RAILWAYS 1931

Legend:

- ▬▬▬ Chinese Eastern Railway
- ▭▭▭ South Manchurian   „
- ━━━ Chinese Railways
- ┼┼┼ Japanese Railways
- ▵▵▵ Russian   „
- ∿∿∿ Rivers
- ━·━·━ State Boundaries

Map labels: CHITA, U.S.S.R., MONGOLIA, MANCHULI, Dauria, HAILAR, Shilka, Argun, GREAT KHINGAN MTS., Nonni, LITTLE KHINGAN MTS., Amur, Blagoveshchensk, KHABA-ROVSK, Heilung Kiang, KOSHAN, HAILUN, TSITSIHAR, Sunghwa Kiang (Sungari), HARBIN, KENTETALIN, Ussuri, CHAHAR, HSINKING, KIRIN, Lao ha ho, LIAO-YUAN, TUNHWA, Vladivostok, Liao ho, HAILUNG, (MUKDEN) FENGTIEN, Yuki, Seishin, Changkiakow Kalgan, PEIPIAO, CHENG-TEH, Peiping, ANT-UNG, Singishu, Gensan, Tientsin, Ryojun (Port Arthur), Dairen, CHOSEN (KOREA), CHINA, Keijo (Soeul)

Scale: 0 — 100 — M. 200

MANCHUKUO

Russia retained the continuation of the Trans-Siberian Railway across North Manchuria (known as the Chinese Eastern Railway—C.E.R.) and the branch from Harbin to the Yellow Sea as far south as Changchun now (Hsinking), while Japan took over the section from Changchun to the port of Dalny (now Dairen). The Japanese line was given the name of the South Manchuria Railway (S.M.R.); it was operated by a company in which the Japanese government owned half the shares and appointed to the highest posts, while the other half of the shares were held mainly by a ring of the biggest family trusts—the so-called *Zaibatsu*. The C.E.R. was always before 1917 under the control of the Russian Ministry of Finance, and from 1924 to 1935 it was the Soviet government which inherited in a modified form the rights of the former Russian company. Both Japan and Russia were therefore deeply involved as states in the affairs of the Manchurian railways, and every transaction of the railway companies tended to become a political issue.

By the treaties and notes of 1915, imposed on China in sequel to the famous "Twenty-one Demands," the terms of Japanese possession of the Kwantung Leased Territory and of the S.M.R. and Antung-Mukden Railway[1] were extended from twenty-five to ninety-nine years from the original dates. Because of the duress under which the concessions were made, the Chinese, in the words of the Lytton Report,[2] "continuously denied that these [the 1915 treaties and notes] were binding upon them." They demanded the abrogation of the 1915 agreements at the Paris Peace Conference in 1919, at the Washington

[1] The Antung-Mukden line linked the S.M.R. with the Japanese railway system in Korea.

[2] *Appeal by the Chinese Government: Report of the Commission of Enquiry*, Geneva, 1932, pp. 49-50.

Conference in 1921-2, and in a note to Japan in 1923; they maintained, as German nationalists held with regard to the Versailles "Diktat," that the treaties lacked "fundamental validity" and so—again to quote the Lytton Report—"they declined to carry out the provisions relating to Manchuria except in so far as circumstances made it expedient to do so." Circumstances meant, in the first place, the Japanese military units stationed in Kwantung and along the S.M.R. as "railway guards"—a force with a separate command known as the Kwantung Army.

The C.E.R. was less obnoxious to Chinese nationalists than the S.M.R., but it also was a cause of trouble, especially after the break between Chiang Kai-shek and the Communists in China in 1927. There were no longer any Russian railway guards on the C.E.R. after 1917, and under the Sino-Soviet agreement of 1924 the Chinese participated in the operation of the line. The Russians, however, retained an effective control and made a political use of it, as in 1925, when they supported the revolt of General Kuo Sung-lin against the Manchurian government of Chang Tso-lin.

After Manchuria's acknowledgment of the Nanking government (controlled by the Kuomintang or "Nationalist" party) as the central government of China, the conflicts of Manchurian railway politics came to a head in the two armed clashes of 1929 and 1931. In the first of these crises the Manchurian Chinese authorities seized the C.E.R. properties, alleging the use of the company offices for Communist propaganda; the Soviet Union responded by concentrating an army on the Manchurian border, invading Manchuria, and compelling the Chinese to restore the *status quo ante* on the railway. The violence in 1931 was wider in scope because the threat to the S.M.R. came, not from direct action, as in the case of the C.E.R., but from a system of Chinese-operated lines designed with the aid of through-traffic arrangements and rate-cutting to divert trade from the S.M.R. and Dairen to a Chinese port—Yingkow (Newchwang) or Hulutao on the Gulf of Liaotung.[1] Up to 1929 the S.M.R. had earned monopoly profits from the economic development of South Manchuria, but from that year the intensive state-organized competition of the Chinese lines began to make big inroads on the profitability of the Japanese system and produced a strong demand for a "positive policy" in Japanese financial circles. The result was the campaign of the Kwantung Army beginning with "the Incident" of 18 September 1931. At the outset Japanese official and public opinion was divided as to the aims of policy to be pursued in Manchuria, and a compromise settlement with the existing Manchurian authorities, preserving at least the nominal sovereignty of China, was possible up to the end of the year. But the exaltation of easy military success, the growth of a reactionary chauvinist movement inside Japan, and anger at the Chinese refusal to enter into bilateral negotiations[2] combined to persuade the rulers of Japan to adopt the policy of setting up a separate sovereign state under Japanese military protection in Manchuria.

[1] Some of the Chinese lines had been financed by the S.M.R. as "feeders," but, having been linked up in the Chinese system, reduced instead of increasing its traffic. The Ssupingkai-Anganchi and Mukden-Kirin were tapped by the Peking-Mukden and Tahushan-Tungliao-Liaoyuan lines.

[2] The Soviet Union, not being a member of the League of Nations in 1929, insisted on bilateral negotiations and declined to admit any kind of mediation. In 1931 China appealed to the League, and Japan, as a member, could not refuse to plead, though she subsequently disregarded the League's verdict.

MANCHUKUO

A number of more or less eminent Chinese of Manchuria and certain Mongol princes lent themselves to this scheme, and a Declaration of Independence was published by them on 18 February 1932; the new state, having taken over the civil administration with the assistance of Japanese advisers, was recognized *de jure* by Japan six months later. Recognition was accompanied by a treaty which empowered Japan to station troops throughout the country for the defense of its newly established sovereignty; the Kwantung Army, which had brought Manchukuo into being, thus obtained the right of permanent occupation.

Manchukuo is provided with a monarchy and Chinese ministers and officials, the throne being held by the heir of the Ch'ing (Manchu) dynasty overthrown in China by the revolution of 1911. The substance of power, however, belongs to the commander-in-chief of the Kwantung Army, who is also Japanese ambassador to Manchukuo, and thus performs the function of a resident or high commissioner in a protectorate. He resides at Hsinking, formerly Changchun, which is now both the capital of Manchukuo and the headquarters of the Kwantung Army. The central administration of Manchuria was removed from Mukden to Changchun to mark the change of regime, and the latter was almost entirely rebuilt to give it the aspect and facilities of a capital city; at the same time the four old provinces of Liaoning, Kirin, Heilungkiang and Jehol were split up to make new divisions with new names, so that the political map of the country has been quite transformed since 1931 (see map 18).

By the action of 1931 the Japanese not only averted the danger to the S.M.R. from politically promoted Chinese competition, but were able themselves to obtain control of the Chinese-operated railways and unite them with the S.M.R. in a single system. Nor was the victory of the S.M.R. restricted to its former domain in South Manchuria. Just two months after the Mukden incident a Japanese column occupied Tsitsihar in Heilung-kiang, thus cutting across the Soviet-controlled C.E.R. The Soviet Union, paralyzed for the time being by the stresses of the First Five-Year Plan, could not risk military counter-measures, and remained passive while the Kwantung Army took possession of North Manchuria up to the Amur. The potential strategic value of the C.E.R. as a short cut to Vladivostok having been destroyed by the Japanese advance, the Soviet government decided to cut its losses, and finally sold its interest in the C.E.R. to Manchukuo in 1935.

With the acquisition of the C.E.R. all the railways of Manchuria came under a unified Japanese management. There was in 1931 a total railway mileage of 4,000; over 2,000 miles of new lines have been constructed since then by the Japanese. Three of the new railways have special strategic, as well as economic, significance. One continues the Dairen-Harbin line north to Heiho on the Amur opposite the Russian town of Blagoveshchensk; a second supplements the old Peking-Mukden line by an inland route *via* Jehol (completed early this year); and a third runs from Rashin on the Korean coast a little way south of the Siberian border to Hsinking, with branches north to Harbin and to Sanchiang province, thus giving Japan railway access to Manchuria from the Japan Sea as well as from the Yellow Sea.

Before 1931 Japan had land frontiers with the Soviet Union only in Karafuto and for a very short stretch in the extreme

16. MANCHURIAN RAILWAYS 1938

NOTE ON MAP 17

Vladivostok was founded on an uninhabited site in 1860; Rashin has been developed from a fishing village into a major port within the last five years. Between Yuki and Kunju the railway from Rashin into Manchukuo runs close to the south-western extremity of Soviet territory. Serious fighting took place for ten days from 29 July 1938 over rival claims to the hill of Changkufeng between the Tumen river and Lake Khasan. The Russians claim that the map attached to a Russo-Chinese border-demarcation treaty of 1886 shows that the hill belongs to them, though it is not apparently marked by name on this map; the Japanese protest that this map was never communicated to Japan with other Russo-Chinese secret agreements at the time of the *entente* of 1911 and that maps prepared by the Russian Imperial General Staff leave the hill on the Chinese side of the frontier. It seems that a serious attempt is now being made to arrive at a final demarcation of the boundary in this area.

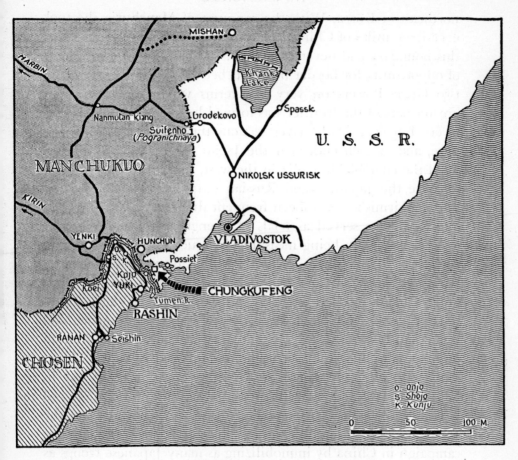

17. VLADIVOSTOK AND RASHIN

northeast of Korea. With the conquest of Manchuria she took
over 1,500 miles of China's Siberian boundary, and the fact that
this boundary had never been precisely demarcated gave plenty
of opportunity for border incidents between the armed forces of
two Great Powers on very bad terms with each other. The
greater part of the frontier was formed by the Amur and Ussuri
rivers, but even in the river sections there were islands in dispute, and at each end, near the Japan Sea in the east and toward the edge of Mongolia in the west, there were no rivers to
separate the Japanese and Russian outposts. In these circumstances skirmishes have been frequent during the last few years
and they have served as trials of strength, willingness to risk
general hostilities being measured by truculence of attitude in
each case. In June 1937 a fight broke out over possession of an
island in the Amur and the Russians withdrew after losing a
gunboat sunk by shell fire; this was soon after the execution of
Tukhachevsky and other Red Army generals in Moscow, and
the Japanese army leaders were encouraged by the exhibition
of Russian weakness to bring matters to a head in North China.
This year, with the Japanese deeply involved in their war in
China, the tables have been turned on the Siberian border, and
it is now the turn of the Russians to press menacingly on the
Japanese. The aim of Soviet policy is to embarrass the Japanese
campaign in China by immobilizing as many Japanese troops as
possible on the Manchukuo border; strategically the most sensi-
tive spot on the line for Japan (though not for Russia) is
where the tongue of Russian territory along the coast southwest of Vladivostok approaches Japan's new artery of communication with Manchukuo, the Rashin-Harbin railway. It is at
this point that fighting has recently been going on. (See map 17
and note.)

MANCHUKUO

The Kwantung Army has a scheme for settling Japanese emigrants, mostly ex-service men, in the provinces of Heiho and Sanchiang near the Amur; there is still much unoccupied land in the far north of Manchuria, and it is here that there is most need for a co-national rural population to support the military garrisons. The scheme provides for the settlement of a million families in twenty years from 1936. So far Japanese colonization in these regions has not prospered, for the conditions of life are very different from those in Japan, and financial assistance for the settlers is likely to be exiguous in the near future, whatever the outcome of the war in China.

As yet only about ten per cent of the population of Manchukuo is to be found in the northern half of the country. Economic life is still concentrated in the south near the Yellow Sea. Here is not only the richest and most closely settled agricultural land, with wheat and soya beans as its main products, but also the Mukden industrial area based on the coal and iron ore of Fengtien province. The center of coal production is at Fushun, a little way to the east of Mukden; to the south is Anshan, site of the Showa Steel Works, now Japan's largest heavy industrial plant. The development of this industrial area under complete Japanese control has undoubtedly strengthened Japan both from an economic and from a military point of view. Fengtien heavy industry is, however, subject to certain drawbacks which cannot be eliminated either by political control or administrative energy. Manchuria has large coal reserves, but is deficient in good coking coal for metallurgical purposes, and its abundant iron ore is almost everywhere of low grade and costly to work. Good coking coal, on the other hand, is produced in Hopei and Shantung in North China, and fairly large reserves of high-grade iron ore exist in Chahar to the west of Jehol. The Japanese occupation of Manchuria thus left China still with a great potential advantage in heavy industry and all it implies, if she were to undertake seriously the exploitation of her coal and iron resources. Such considerations counted for much in persuading the Kwantung Army to extend the "manifest destiny" from Manchuria to Inner Mongolia and North China.

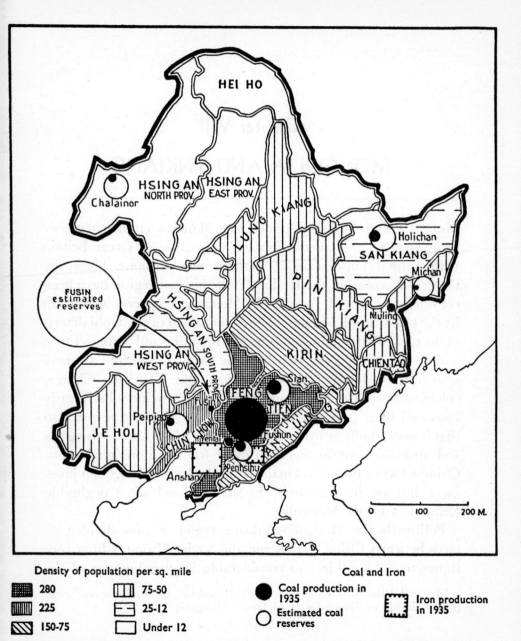

HEI HO

HSING AN
NORTH PROV.
Chalainor

HSING AN
EAST PROV.

LUNG KIANG

SAN KIANG
Holichan

Michan

FUSIN
estimated
reserves

HSING AN SOUTH PROV.

PIN KIANG

Muling

HSING AN
WEST PROV.

KIRIN

CHIENTAO

Sian

FENG TIEN

Fusi

JE HOL

Peipiao

CHIN CHOW

Yenta

AN TUNG

Fushun

Penhsihu

Anshan

Density of population per sq. mile

▦ 280   ▥ 75-50

▨ 225   ☰ 25-12

◩ 150-75   ▢ Under 12

Coal and Iron

● Coal production in 1935

○ Estimated coal reserves

▢ Iron production in 1935

18. MANCHUKUO: COAL, IRON AND DENSITY OF POPULATION

Chapter VIII

MONGOLIA AND SINKIANG

Mongolia and Sinkiang under the Manchu empire together comprised an area about eighteen times that of Great Britain with a total population of perhaps five millions. Since the Chinese Revolution the landmarks of this vast region have been considerably altered, for the old Mongolia has been broken up by the constitution in Outer Mongolia (north of the Gobi desert) of the two independent republics of Mongolia[1] and Tannu-Tuva, and in Inner Mongolia (south of the Gobi) of the four Chinese provinces of Jehol, Chahar, Suiyüan and Ninghsia. Chinese colonization in the four Inner Mongolian provinces has greatly increased their population during the last twenty-five years, so that it now stands at over seven millions, while Outer Mongolia and Sinkiang contain together about four million inhabitants. Chinese form a numerical majority in the Inner Mongolian provinces, but are in a minority in Sinkiang and are a negligible element in Outer Mongolia.

Politically the Mongolia-Sinkiang region is now divided *de facto* between China, Japan and the Soviet Union. China continues to hold, subject to considerable insubordination of the

[1] In full title the Mongol People's Republic; often, however, mentioned simply as Mongolia or as Outer Mongolia.

provincial governors, Ninghsia and Sinkiang. Japan incorporated Jehol in Manchukuo in 1933, and has overrun Chahar and part of Suiyüan in the campaign of 1937-8, setting up an "autonomous" Mongol state to the southwest of Manchukuo. The Soviet Union holds under a kind of protectorate Outer Mongolia and Tannu-Tuva, which were originally detached from China in 1912.

The predominant characteristic of both Mongolia and Sinkiang is aridity. About ninety-five per cent of the total area is either desert of sand or gravel, or grassland, good for pasture but incapable of cultivation. Arable land is found only in the south near the Great Wall, where the summer monsoons from the south bring some rain; in the valleys of the Altai and Sayan, which get their rainfall by westerly winds from the Atlantic; and at the foot of the T'ien-shan ranges, where streams fed by the snows of the high peaks can be used for irrigation in places where there is little or no rainfall. In Sinkiang there is more true desert than in Mongolia, but irrigated cultivation has been carried on in the oases from early times, so that the sedentary element of population has always been stronger relatively than in Mongolia, where most of the land is of the type intermediate between desert and arable and is well suited to an economy of nomadic herdsmen.

The main desert belt is formed by the Taklamakan, Kum Tagh and Gobi tracts stretching east-northeast from Yarkand to the Great Khingan. Outer Mongolia and Sinkiang lie on the farther side of this belt, and Inner Mongolia on the nearer side, as approached from China. A "line of enormous sandhills"[1] marks the actual boundary between Inner and Outer Mongolia

[1] Sir Eric Teichman, *Journey to Turkestan*, p. 49.

to the north of the Suiyüan-Hami motor caravan route, and the Gobi desert as a whole is a natural frontier of great impenetrability. It cuts off Outer Mongolia and Sinkiang from China while leaving them in close contact with the territories of the Soviet Union to the north and west. It is not surprising, therefore, that China should have found it difficult to hold under her authority the conquests of the Manchu empire on the other side of the "sea of sand," and that Soviet influence should be paramount there, though with different effect at Urga and at Urumchi. Inner Mongolia, on the other hand, is well within China's reach, and would by now be firmly held by the Nanking government were it not for the Japanese penetration westward from South Manchuria.

Apart from the Chinese there are three nationality elements in the Mongolia-Sinkiang region. The Mongols are scattered all over Mongolia, except for Tannu-Tuva, and are also represented in the former "Three Eastern Provinces" (Manchuria), in central Sinkiang (the Kalmuk enclave north of Karashar) and in Tsinghai to the south of the Kansu Chinese corridor; they speak various dialects of the Mongol language, and are all traditionally nomads by culture and Lama-Buddhists by religion. There are between four and five millions of them in all, and fully three-quarters of them numerically live in Manchuria and Inner Mongolia, but their numbers in these areas are inferior to the masses of Chinese in close proximity, so that Outer Mongolia, which is thoroughly Mongol, has for long been the national base.

To the northwest of Mongolia between the Sayan and Tannuola mountains dwell the Uriankhai, a very primitive people speaking a Turki language; they only number some 50,000, but

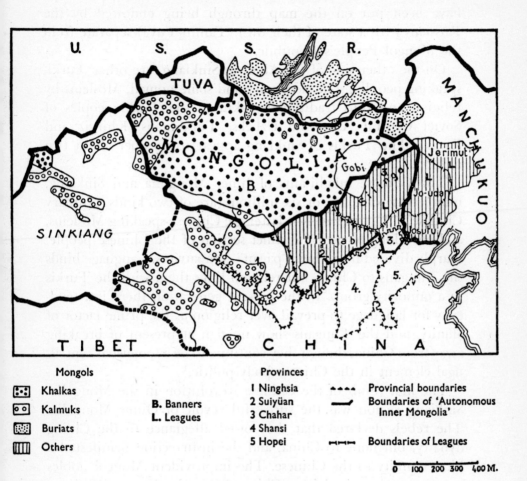

Mongols

	Khalkas
	Kalmuks
	Buriats
	Others

B. Banners
L. Leagues

Provinces

1 Ninghsia
2 Suiyüan
3 Chahar
4 Shansi
5 Hopei

•••• Provincial boundaries
━━━ Boundaries of 'Autonomous Inner Mongolia'
┝━┥ Boundaries of Leagues

0 100 200 300 400 M.

19. THE MONGOLS

have been put on the map through being endowed by the Russians with a state of their own (Tannu-Tuva) separate from the Mongol People's Republic.

On the other side of the Altai, in Sinkiang, are other Turki-speaking peoples, some sedentary and some nomad, Moslems by religion and thus traditionally akin to the Turki peoples of Soviet Central Asia—the Uzbeks, Turkomans, Khirgiz and Kazaks. The Turkis of Sinkiang appear to number about two million.

The Chinese inhabitants of Inner Mongolia and Sinkiang, numbering some five or six millions, are of two kinds, ordinary Chinese and Tungans. The latter are Chinese-speaking Moslems, and have long formed a distinct section of the Chinese people, sharply divided from their "pagan" compatriots. Language binds the Tungans to China, but religion links them with the Turkis in a minority group. In the present generation there is a tendency for language to prevail over religion as the prime factor of affinity, and the Tungans show no sign at present of breaking away from China, though they continue to be a somewhat centrifugal element in the Chinese body politic.[1]

The first result of the Chinese Revolution in the Mongolia-Sinkiang region was the successful revolt of Outer Mongolia. The rebels declared that they owed allegiance to the Ch'ing dynasty, but none to China, and the insurrection manifested a bitter enmity to the Chinese. The improvident Mongol nobles were everywhere in debt to Chinese moneylenders, and Chinese peasant settlers were continually encroaching on the pastures of the Mongol tribes to the north of the Great Wall. The inde-

[1] See page 60 on the symbolism of the five-barred Republican flag which counted the Moslems as a "nation."

pendence movement was general in both Inner and Outer Mongolia; that it failed in the former region, while succeeding in the latter, was due not only to the advantages the rebels derived from the remoteness of Outer Mongolia and the barrier of the Gobi desert, but also to other factors. The old tribal organization of the Mongols had been preserved much better in Outer, than in Inner, Mongolia. The Mongols were divided into numerous "banners" (*hoshun*) grouped into confederacies (*aimak*); of the latter there were only four in Outer, but twenty-four in Inner, Mongolia. The Inner Mongols were thus more split up than their kinsmen beyond the Gobi, and Peking governmental control over them was further increased by a system of artificial combinations called "leagues" (*chiguglan*). As many of the banner princes also found profit in selling tribal lands to Chinese settlers, Chinese domination in Inner Mongolia was too strong to be broken down before the arrival of the Japanese.

The Mongol revolt in Outer Mongolia in 1912 was supported by Russia, who extorted from China recognition of Outer Mongolian autonomy under nominal Chinese sovereignty. The Russians at the same time made claims to the Uriankhai territory, now Tannu-Tuva, and secured its separation from Mongolia; after the outbreak of the Great War in 1914 it was brought under direct Russian administration. Russian power, however, dwindled after the revolution of 1917, and the Chinese took the opportunity to send an expedition across the Gobi and capture Urga, the capital of autonomous Outer Mongolia. The Mongol princes called to their aid a White Russian force under Baron Ungern von Sternberg, who drove out the Chinese, but was himself overthrown by a Red Russian column pursuing him from Siberia. The new Soviet Russia renewed the independence of Outer Mongolia *vis-à-vis* China, but transformed its institutions with the aid of a revolutionary party among the Mongols. Power had been in the hands of the banner princes with the Buddhist metropolitan of Urga, the Khutukhtu or "Living Buddha," as the head of the state; this regime was replaced in 1924 by the Mongol People's Republic with a popular national assembly as the legal sovereign. Tannu-Tuva had meanwhile been proclaimed a separate republic, the Russian colonists there being locally the most important element.

China has not had any control over the governments of Outer Mongolia or Tannu-Tuva for the last seventeen years, and these states have external relations only with the Soviet Union, with which they have concluded military alliances. Chinese sovereignty over all this territory is still, however, juridically recognized by all other states, including the Soviet Union, and the new republics have not claimed sovereignty as Manchukuo has done, though they are quite as effectively removed from the jurisdiction of the central government of China. The principal reason appears to be that the Mongol and Uriankhai states and their Soviet Union protectors are content with the fact of separation and are willing to leave the empty form of sovereignty to China, whereas the restored Manchu monarchy in Hsinking cannot acknowledge even nominally the supremacy of the Chinese Republic.

The Soviet Union does not have to keep an army of occupation in Outer Mongolia to prevent it from rejoining China of its own volition, for Mongol nationalism can be relied on to resist Chinese overtures. The social radicalism of the People's Republic has, however, alienated the formerly privileged noble and priestly classes and thus split the national independence movement into two factions, both anti-Chinese, but looking to different quarters for support. The "Red" Mongols rely on the Soviet Union to sustain their cause, but the more conservative nationalists in Inner Mongolia, anxious to free themselves from the Chinese yoke, and yet afraid to accept aid from the "City of the Red Heroes" (Ulan Bator Khoto—Urga, as renamed in 1924), turned to Japan when the columns of the Kwantung Army broke out from the Japanese railway zone of Manchuria across the Chinese-inhabited corn-lands to the Mongol steppe.

The Japanese were not slow to realize the value of an alliance with Mongol nationalism. No real separatism could be induced among the Chinese of Manchuria, but the anti-Chinese sentiment of the Mongols made them an ideal instrument for Japanese imperialism. The Mongol-inhabited western parts of Manchuria, including northern Jehol, were therefore detached and made into a new province called Hsingan (subsequently divided into four: North, East, West and South Hsingan), and the Mongols were given a special status and guarantees against Chinese officialdom in the new state structure of Manchukuo. The Japanese have not been entirely successful, however, in winning the support of the Manchukuo Mongols, for the economic urges of their imperialism have prevented them from leaving the Mongols alone to continue in their old ways of life. From the point of view of Japanese economy Hsingan is of great potential value as a producer of wool within the Japanese currency area; in time it might free the Japanese wool industry from dependence on imports from Australia. But the wool hitherto produced by the Mongol nomads is too coarse to be suitable for industrial purposes, and Japanese attempts to improve the breed of sheep have involved a degree of administrative interference and compulsion much resented by the Mongols.

MONGOLIA AND SINKIANG

The condition of the Mongols in Manchukuo was nevertheless greatly preferable to that of their kinsmen in Chahar and Suiyüan who remained under Chinese rule until 1937. The Chinese officials there continued to enclose Mongol tribal lands and sell or rent them to Chinese settlers from the south. In 1936 there was a Mongol revolt under the leadership of Prince Teh; the Kwantung Army supplied the rebels with munitions, but was restrained by the Tokyo government from serious intervention, and Teh was defeated. In the following year, however, after the Lukouchiao incident had precipitated general hostilities against China, the Kwantung Army overran Chahar and Suiyüan as far as the terminus of the railway from Peiping at Paotou on the great northward bend of the Yellow River. An autonomous Mongol state covering the two provinces was then proclaimed under the name of Mêng Chiang.

The great economic importance of Chahar lies in its deposits of high-grade iron ore, which are located about 150 miles northwest of Peiping. As this area is so closely connected with Hopei, consideration of it will be deferred to the next chapter; it suffices to point out here that control of the iron ore of Chahar has been one of the principal objectives of Japan's North China policy ever since the completion of the conquest of Manchuria in 1933.

By her advance westward into Inner Mongolia Japan has intercepted the old Russia-China trade route *via* Urga and Kalgan and also that *via* Hami and Suiyüan. But the Soviet Union, Outer Mongolia, the Chinese Communists in Kansu and Shensi and the Kuomintang central government of China have now all been brought into a combination against Japan, and they are in contact by routes which remain out of reach of the Japanese.

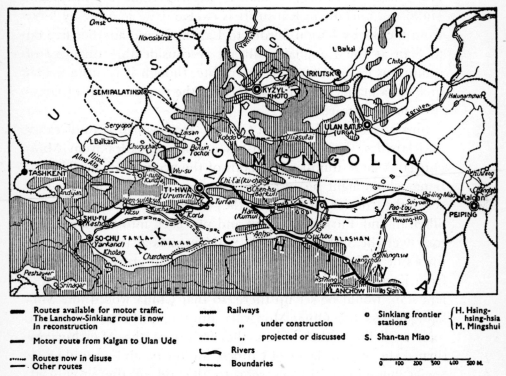

Routes available for motor traffic. The Lanchow-Sinkiang route is now in reconstruction

Motor route from Kalgan to Ulan Ude

Routes now in disuse
Other routes

Railways

"   under construction

"   projected or discussed

Rivers

Boundaries

Sinkiang frontier stations
{ H. Hsing-hsing-hsia
  M. Mingshui }

S. Shan-tan Miao

0   100   200   300   400   500 M.

20. MONGOLIA AND SINKIANG: COMMUNICATIONS

One is a trail across the desert from Urga to Ninghsia; another, much more important, is the dirt road by Urumchi (Tihwa) and Hami to Lanchow in Kansu. It is twelve days' journey by lorry from the Soviet Union border to Lanchow, and another five on to Sian at the Lunghai railhead. A considerable quantity of munitions enters China by this route, though it is quite inadequate as a main channel of supply for the requirements of large-scale modern warfare.[1]

Sinkiang is now held by a Chinese army which is implacably anti-Japanese because it consists mainly of exiles from Manchuria. A large number of troops of the army of Chang Hsüeh-liang who fought against the Japanese in 1931-2 finally fled across the frontier into Siberia; they were conveyed by the Trans-Siberian and Turksib railways and put back into Chinese territory over the Sinkiang border. Sinkiang was at the time in the throes of a Turki rebellion supported by an army of Tungans from Kansu, and it appeared likely that an independent Moslem state would be set up there, so that China would lose Sinkiang no less than Outer Mongolia. But the Turkis and Tungans took to fighting each other, the arrival of the Manchurians turned the scale in favor of Chinese authority, and a number of Soviet bombing airplanes sent to the aid of the provincial government settled the matter. The great Moslem revolt collapsed in 1934. It may be noted that Soviet policy in Sinkiang was the opposite to what it was in Outer Mongolia; in the latter region the Russians sustained Mongol separatism against China, while in the former they helped the Chinese to crush a separatist national insurrection. The reason was no doubt fear of the

[1] The greater part of the Russian munition supply to China goes from Odessa to Canton by sea.

attraction which an independent Turki Moslem state in Sinkiang might have for the ex-Moslem Soviet citizens of Kazakstan, Khirgizia and Uzbekistan. The capitulation of the Turkis and the retreat of the Tungans left Sinkiang under the rule of an energetic Chinese general who owed his position to support from Moscow, who stood for anti-Japanism in an extreme form, and who could not be a cause of unrest in Soviet Central Asia.

Chapter IX

SOUTH OF THE WALL

Of the eighteen provinces of China Proper—often known simply as the Eighteen Provinces (*shih pa shêng*)—five are of primary importance, holding key positions at the center and at the four points of the compass respectively. These five contain, or contained two years ago, the seven most populous cities in China,[1] as shown in the following table:

		Province	*Cities*
North	. . .	Hopei	Peiping, Tientsin
East	. . .	Kiangsu	Shanghai, Nanking
Center	. . .	Hupeh	Hankow
West	. . .	Szechwan	Chungking
South	. . .	Kwangtung	Canton

The five key provinces are linked together by China's two

[1] The figures as given by the *Chinese Year Book* of 1935-6 (not applicable today in view of mass exodus from places in the war zone) are as follows:

(1) Shanghai	- -	3,259,114	(5) Hankow	- -	777,993
(2) Peiping	- -	1,496,648	(6) Nanking	- -	681,855
(3) Tientsin	- -	1,387,462	(7) Chungking	- -	635,000
(4) Canton	- -	1,122,583			

The only other towns given as possessing more than 600,000 inhabitants are Changsha in Hunan, and Wenchow in Chekiang.

114

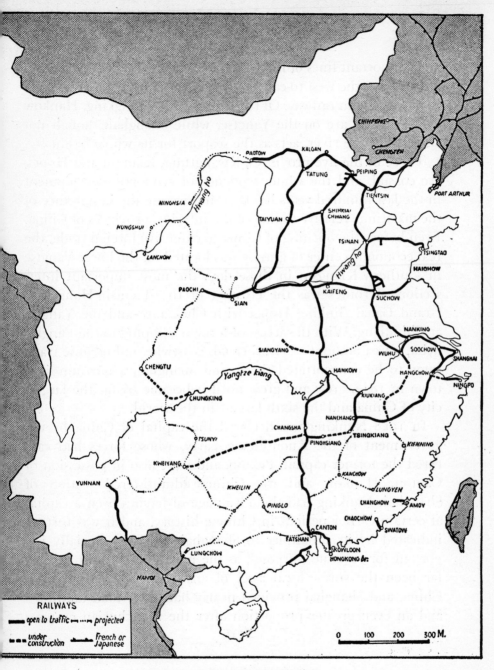

21. CHINA: RAILWAYS

RAILWAYS
— open to traffic ···· projected
— — under construction —•— French or Japanese

0   100   200   300 M.

most important lines of internal communication, which intersect at Hankow: the west-to-east Yangtse river and the north-to-south Peiping-Canton railway. Of the seven cities Chungking, Hankow and Nanking are on the Yangtse, while Shanghai, though not actually on the river, acts as the seaport for its whole basin.

Three of the five provinces, Kwangtung, Kiangsu and Hopei, are coastal, and the whole tendency of economic development in the last hundred years has been to increase the importance of the maritime, relative to that of the interior, provinces of China. Even before the opening of China to extensive foreign trade, the real economic center of gravity was located on the lower Yangtse in southern Kiangsu; in those days the most important inter-section of routes was the crossing of the Tientsin-Hangchow Grand Canal (linking Hopei with Chekiang) and the Yangtse at Chinkiang. With the access of foreign shipping to the Yangtse delta, a vast amount of river, canal, coastwise and oceanic trade came to be concentrated there, and Shanghai, a medium-sized town in 1842, grew and grew until it became by far the largest city of China and the sixth largest in the world.

In 1928 Nanking was declared the capital of China by the government of the Kuomintang party, whose forces had captured the former capital, Peking, and were also in possession of Canton, Hankow and the Chinese-administered section of Shanghai. Nanking had the advantage of having been a capital at certain earlier periods in Chinese history, and it was further indicated by its proximity to Shanghai; this was specially important for revenue purposes, as the maritime customs have so far been the surest fiscal asset of any central government in China, and Shanghai provided nearly half their total takings— and an even greater proportion after the Manchurian customs

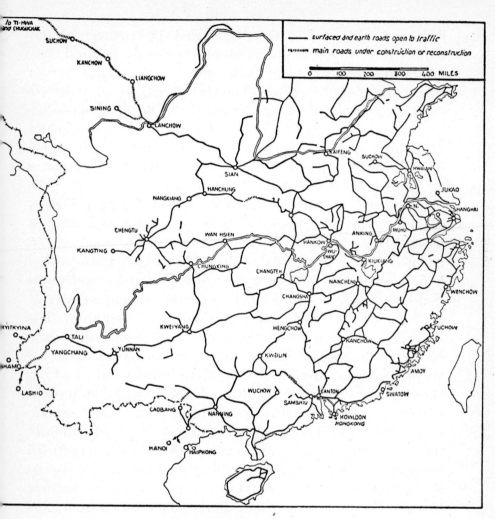

To TI-HWA
and CHUGUCHAK

SUCHOW

KANCHOW

LIANGCHOW

SINING

LANCHOW

surfaced and earth roads open to traffic

main roads under construction or reconstruction

0   100   200   300   400 MILES

KAIFENG

SUCHOW

HWAIAN

SIAN

HANCHUNG

JUKAO

NANGKIANG

N.

SHANGHAI

CHENGTU

WAN HSIEN

ANKING

WUHU

HANKOW

KANGTING

WU
CHANG

KIUKIANG

CHUNGKING

CHANGTEH

NANCHENG

WENCHOW

CHANGSHA

MYITKYINA

TALI

KWEIYANG

HENGCHOW

KANCHOW

FUCHOW

YANGCHANG

YUNNAN

BHAMO

KWEILIN

AMOY

LASHIO

WUCHOW

CANTON

SWATOW

CAOBANG

SAMSHIU

NANNING

KOWLOON
HONGKONG

HANOI

HAIPHONG

22. CHINA: ROADS

had been subtracted in 1932.[1] Shanghai, the commercial and industrial metropolis, could not itself become the political capital, because half of it was under foreign administration (the International Settlement and French Concession).

As already pointed out in Chapter II, the Yellow River valley was the original seat of Chinese civilization, and the Yangtse valley long remained a country of forest and swamp with savage inhabitants. But the basin of the Yangtse not only contains a larger area of cultivable land than that of the Yellow River; the Yangtse itself, the fourth river of the world in length, is navigable for 2,000 miles from the sea, whereas the Yellow River is blocked by rapids in its upper, and by shoals and sandbanks in its lower course, so as to be of little use for navigation. As the Yangtse valley was brought under cultivation and long-distance trade increased, it was inevitable that the economic center of gravity in China should tend to shift southward from the Yellow River; the center of political power, however, remained usually in the north, mainly because the central government had to attend to the ever troublesome northern frontier and could not afford to be too far away from it, while the Mongol and Manchu conquerors of China naturally sought to exert their dominion from a point which was convenient for organizing the administration of China, but also within easy reach of their own northern homelands. Such a point was Peiping, the Cambaluc of Kublai Khan, in the extreme north of China Proper, but about halfway between Canton and the Amur. Except for a period from 1368 to 1421 when Nanking was the capital, the Yüan (Mongol), Ming and Ch'ing (Manchu) dynasties ruled from Peiping —latterly called Peking or "Northern Capital" (1280-1911).

[1] In 1930, St.$ 135 out of 281 millions; in 1934 St.$ 175 out of 335 millions.

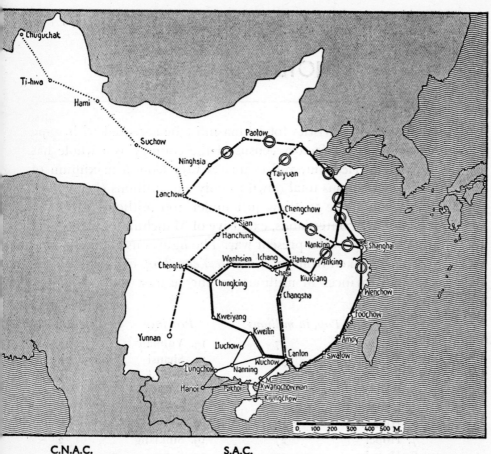

C.N.A.C.
The China National
Aviation Corporation

S.A.C.
The South-western
Aviation Corporation

**Eurasia Aviation
Corporation**

**Eurasia line
temporarily suspended**

**Lines interrupted
by war**

23. CHINA: AIRWAYS

NOTE ON MAP 24

All population statistics for China must be accepted with some reserve, as no satisfactory census of the country as a whole has ever been carried out, and estimates vary from a maximum of nearly 500 millions total down to only 250 millions (Legendre). It is probably safe to allow just under 400 millions for China Proper and the outer lands, exclusive of Manchukuo, at the time of the outbreak of the present war. The figures used for the map opposite are taken from the *Chinese Year Book* of 1937, and the totals by provinces in millions (to the nearest million) are as follows:

Province	*Pop. in millions*	*Province*	*Pop. in millions*
1. Szechwan[1]	47	13. Yunnan	12
2. Shantung	35	14. Shansi	11
3. Honan	33	15. Shensi	10
4. Kiangsu	31	16. Fukien	10
5. Kwangtung	31	17. Kweichow	7
6. Hunan	28	18. Kansu	6
7. Hopei	27	19. Sinkiang	2
8. Hupeh	27	20. Suiyuan	2
9. Anhwei	22	21. Chahar	2
10. Chekiang	20	22. Tsinghai	1
11. Kiangsi	16	23. Sikang	1
12. Kwangsi	13	24. Ninghsia	1

[1] The 1936 edition of the *Chinese Year Book*, however, gives the population of Szechwan as only 37 millions. It has on the other hand been estimated at more than 50 millions.

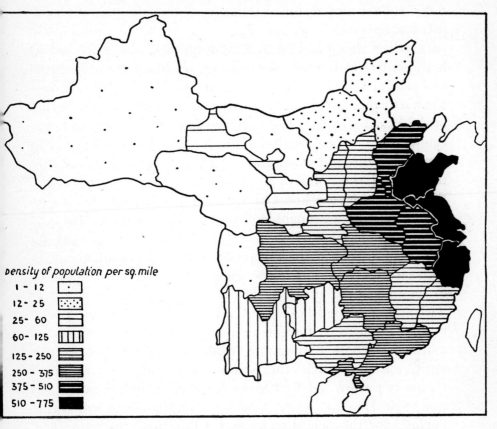

density of population per sq. mile

1 - 12	
12 - 25	
25 - 60	
60 - 125	
125 - 250	
250 - 375	
375 - 510	
510 - 775	

24. CHINA: DENSITY OF POPULATION BY PROVINCES

SOUTH OF THE WALL

After the Republic had replaced the Manchu dynasty Peking remained the capital, but it was now neither the seat of an impressive imperial court nor the center of the new progressive nationalism which had created the Republic. The latter had its headquarters at Canton. Kwangtung, separated from northern and central China by the Nanling mountain range, has always had a strong provincial individuality, and throughout the period of the Manchu dynasty had been the focus of antagonism to the conquering race; in addition to this it had had long contact with Europeans through trade and the emigration of Cantonese to the Dutch Indies, Malaya and California. Thus Canton became the principal base of the Chinese Revolution, while Peking remained in spirit a stronghold of the *ancien régime* even after the collapse of the monarchy.

The spearhead of the revolution was the Kuomintang party with a nucleus of Cantonese politicians who, finding it impossible to consolidate the initial success of the revolution in China as a whole, repudiated Peking and all its works and set up a separate government at Canton in 1917. For nine years the Kuomintang ruled in Kwangtung, while various factions of "war lords" warred on each other in the rest of China; then in 1926 the party's army, led by Chiang Kai-shek, marched north and won, first Hankow, then Nanking and Shanghai, and finally Peking,[1] for the new dispensation. China was thus re-unified, though the new unity was far from complete, by a movement sweeping the country from south to north. It is to be noted that

[1] Peking was not captured by the forces under Chiang Kai-shek, whose advance from Nanking was interrupted by the clash with the Japanese at Tsinan, but by the army of Shansi under Yen Hsi-shan, who threw in his lot with the Kuomintang after their victories on the Yangtse.

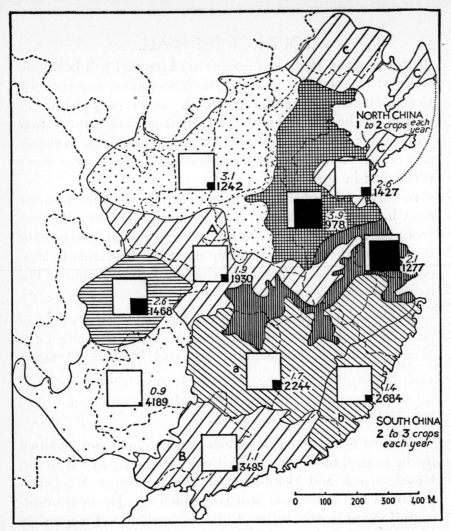

NORTH CHINA
1 to 2 crops each year

3.1
1242

2.6
1427

3.9
978

A

2.1
1277

1.9
1930

2.8
1468

0.9
4189

a

1.7
2244

1.4
2684

B

1.1
3495

b

SOUTH CHINA
2 to 3 crops each year

0   100   200   300   400 M.

DENSITY OF POPULATION PER SQ. MILE AND NAME OF REGION

	897	Yangtse Plain
	647	North China Plain
	581	Red Basin of Szechwan
	421	South Yangtse Hills (a) 417 South-eastern Coast (b)
	290	Central mountain belt (A) 285 Hills of Liangkwang (B)
	286	Mountains of Shantung, Jehol, Liao-tung (C)
	211	Loess Highlands
	157	South-western tableland

CULTIVATED LAND

Percentage of cultivated land (black square) to total area of the region (white square).

3495 Density of population per sq. mile on cultivated land only.

1.1 Area of cultivated land per person (in mow; 100 mow = 16.47 acre).

Figures used to make this map are from G. F. Cressey (*Geographical Foundations of China*). Areas of regions correspond to planometer reading and are adopted from the same work.

25. CHINA: AGRICULTURE

the effect of the Japanese invasion has been and will be, if successful, to reverse this process. The Kuomintang sequence was Canton-Hankow-Shanghai-Peiping; the order of Japanese objectives has been Peiping-Shanghai-Hankow, and if these three focal points are taken and held by the Japanese, the Kuomintang power will be put back into the southern region from which it emerged in 1926.

In the present war the essentially strategic aims of the Japanese must be distinguished from their economic purposes. The advance on Hankow belongs to the former category, whereas the invasions of the Peiping-Tientsin and Shanghai-Nanking areas correspond to the economic motives of Japanese policy. The latter fall under three heads:

(1) To acquire control, within the Japanese currency area, of essential raw materials in which Japan, even after the conquest of Manchuria, is deficient, notably coking coal, iron ore and cotton.

(2) To acquire monopoly or preference in Chinese trade.

(3) To prevent the competitive industrialization of China, both in heavy and light industries.

The first of the above objectives could be sufficiently realized by the control of the "Five Northern Provinces," that is to say, Hopei, Shansi and Shantung plus the two Inner Mongolian provinces of Chahar and Suiyüan, which the Japanese unsuccessfully tried to detach from China by intrigue and menaces in 1935. Aims (2) and (3), on the other hand, required in addition a campaign for domination of Kiangsu, where half the trade of China had its outlet and a formidable Chinese textile industry was growing up in the decade before 1937.

The Five Northern Provinces are economically important,

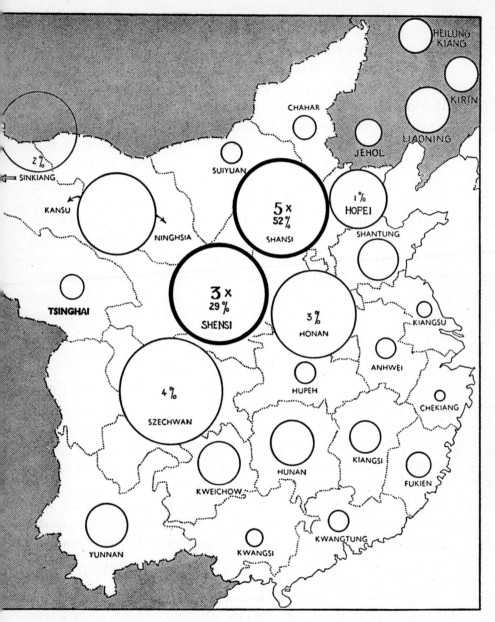

Source : General statement on the Mining Industry in China (National Geological Survey) presented by the Information Bulletin, Council of International Affairs, Nanking.

The circles for Shansi and Shensi are to be enlarged five and three times respectively.

26. CHINA: COAL RESOURCES

not so much for their actual productiveness as for their potential wealth as the region of future location for the biggest heavy industry in the Far East. To quote from a paper read to the World Engineering Congress in 1929:[1] "Disregarding political boundaries, perhaps the best potential combination in the Pacific region [for heavy industry] would be between the iron ores of India or of the Philippines and the Dutch East Indies on the one hand, and the coking coal of the northeastern provinces of China on the other, with smelting centered on the Chinese coast, possibly on the Bay of Pe-chi-li [Po Hai]." In other words, as North China has the best supply of coking coal in the Far East, and as, owing to the relative tonnages involved, iron ore moves to coal rather than the reverse, the seaboard of Hopei is indicated as the best site in the Far East for the growth of a heavy industry. Nor would such an industry be entirely dependent on imports of iron ore from the overseas sources mentioned in the above quotation; the Five Northern Provinces contain not only the principal coking coal deposits of the Far East, but also the "most important single iron ore region in China"[2]—the Hsüan Lung deposits in Chahar estimated at 90 million tons of high grade, or more than the entire estimated reserves of Japan and Korea put together. The Hsüan Lung field lies about 150 miles northwest of Peiping, and its natural outlet is to Hopei, where the Kaiping coalfield supplies coking coal.

To the west of Hopei lies Shansi with more than half of China's estimated probable coal reserve, which is about thirty times Japan's. Because of Shansi's inland seclusion its coal resources

[1] C. K. Leith, "The World's Iron Ore Supply." Quoted by H. Foster Bain, *Ores and Industry in the Far East*, p. 265.
[2] Bain, *Ores and Industry in the Far East*, p. 96.

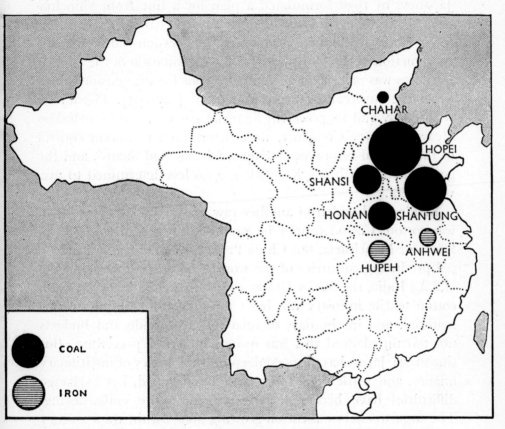

27. CHINA: COAL AND IRON PRODUCTION, 1936

can only be made available with the aid of railways, and the Japanese in 1936 formulated a plan for a line from Shihchia-chwang to Tsangchow to link the Shansi coal mines with the coast. China's refusal to grant Japan concessions either for the construction of this railway or for the exploitation of the Chahar iron ores was one of the principal reasons for the tension which led to the outbreak of war at the end of July 1937. The Kwan-tung Army and its powerful financial partner, the Manchukuo Heavy Industry Company, were determined to obtain control of the mineral resources of Hopei, Chahar and Shansi, and the government of Chiang Kai-shek was no less determined to pre-vent them.

Besides coal and iron another raw material sought by Japan was cotton. Cotton cannot be produced successfully in Japan, Korea or Manchuria, but China Proper is one of the five princi-pal producing countries of the world (the other four being the U.S.A., India, the Soviet Union and Egypt). The great Japanese cotton textile industry was built up entirely on imported raw material, and in the days of relatively free trade and budgets not too unbalanced this was quite a practical procedure. But since 1931 Japan has plunged deep into the mazes of inflationary finance, and while her export trade has boomed, her exchange difficulties have become ever more and more embarrassing. The urge to enclose a cotton-growing area within the currency domain of the yen had become very strong in the Japanese tex-tile industry by 1937. It is an essential part of Japanese expansion to provide conquered regions with a currency tied to the yen, so as to reduce the amount of imports which must be paid for in currencies not under Japanese control. Cotton is produced in western Shantung, Hopei and southern Shansi, so that en-

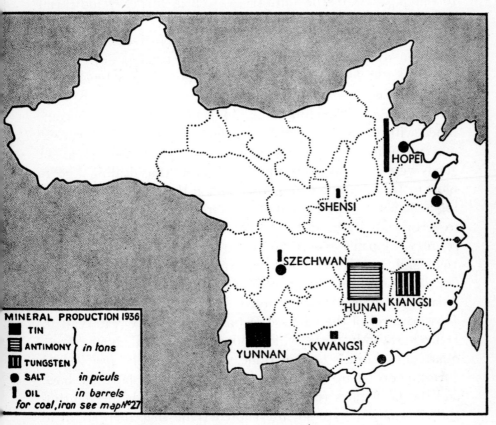

MINERAL PRODUCTION 1936
■ TIN
▤ ANTIMONY } *in tons*
▥ TUNGSTEN
● SALT   *in piculs*
▮ OIL   *in barrels*
for coal, iron see map Nº27

HOPEI

SHENSI

SZECHWAN

HUNAN   KIANGSI

YUNNAN   KWANGSI

28. CHINA: MINERAL PRODUCTION, 1936

closure of the Five Northern Provinces could be of great benefit[1] to the Japanese textile industry as well as to heavy industrial interests.

Apart from raw materials, Japan's principal economic aim has been to reverse the trend of Chinese tariff policy. In the words of the *Japan Year Book* for 1937:[2] "The Manchurian Incident, 1931, enabled Japan to get the lion's share in the foreign trade of Manchukuo . . . but on the other hand, combined with the Shanghai Affair, it intensified the anti-Japanese movement in China. Increases in China's tariffs on Japanese goods were also effected in rapid succession, thus dealing a great blow to Japan's trade with China[3] and at the same time furnishing a chance for the United States, Great Britain and Germany to recover their commercial influence of former years in that country." Japan's exports to China declined in value between 1930 and 1936 (even allowing for subtraction of the Manchurian share from the 1930 figures), while the export total to Asia as a whole almost doubled. The present war has given Japan control of the Chinese seaboard from the Great Wall to Hangchow with ports which normally handle about three-quarters of China's foreign trade, and through the provisional governments set up at Peiping and Nanking the Japanese have had the tariff rates revised in their favor, though the fighting and devastation have so interrupted trade that there is little enough for anyone at the present time.

If the Five Northern Provinces are of supreme importance for

[1] So far this aim has not been realized, as Chinese guerrillas have prevented the marketing of the crop.

[2] P. 424.

[3] The tariffs did not discriminate against Japan by name, but were raised against all types and qualities of goods in which Japan specialized.

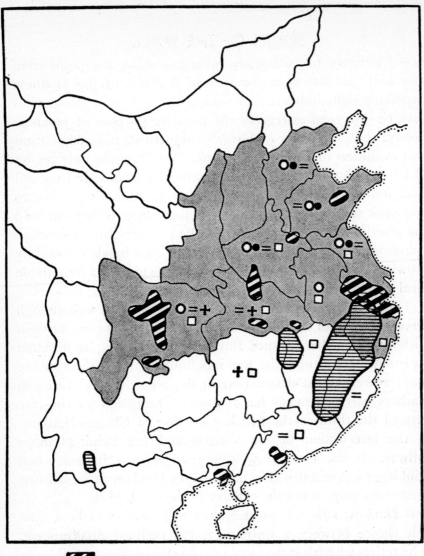

▨ Intensive sericulture	□ Rape seeds
	= Ground nuts
▤ Main cultivation of tea	+ Tung seed
	○ Soya bean
▦ Principal cotton-producing provinces	● Sesame seed

Provinces are shown which have an annual production of vegetable oil of
500,000 piculs minimum

29. CHINA: TEA, SILK, COTTON AND VEGETABLE OIL PRODUCTION

heavy industry raw materials, Shanghai is the key point commercially and has been the special objective of the Japanese exporting light industries. A similar distinction of group aims may be discerned as regards the negative purpose of Japanese policy: the prevention of China's competitive industrialization and evolution to Great Power rank. By seizing the only region of China suitable for the development of a large-scale iron and steel industry, the Japanese have thwarted China's advance to economic supremacy in the Far East for as long as they can hold the positions they have gained; by the capture of the Shanghai-Nanking area they have taken into their own hands the rapidly growing Chinese cotton industry, which was already a formidable rival to the mills of Osaka and Kobe.

The economic ends of Japanese policy would be well enough served by control of the Five Northern Provinces plus Kiangsu without any further advance. But as the Kuomintang has declared its resolve to continue the war indefinitely, and as the Chinese main army escaped destruction in the Shanghai and Lunghai Railway battles, strategy has required a campaign for the capture of the third of the five key districts of China—Hankow, at the intersection of the Yangtse and the Peiping-Canton railway. At the time of writing the Japanese have reached Kiukiang; it is said that they hope to take Hankow in September, or alternatively, to cut the railway to the south of it.

If Hankow falls, Chiang Kai-shek will have to make a difficult choice between a military and a political disadvantage. If he retires with his main force into Szechwan, he will still be in a central position as between the southern and northwestern provinces not yet invaded, but his army will suffer from a shortage of military supplies, as Szechwan will no longer have rail and

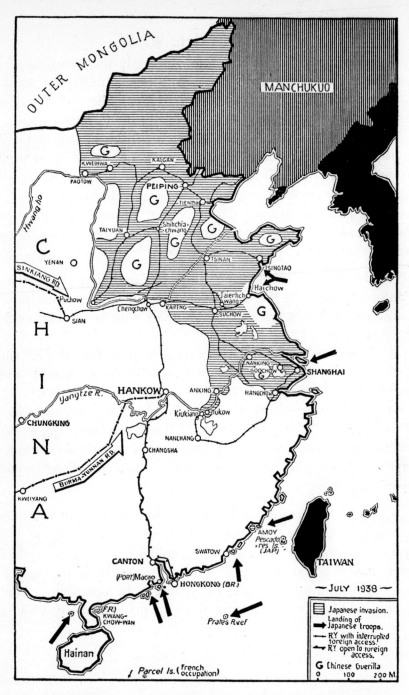

30. CHINA: THE JAPANESE INVASION, 1937-38

river communication with Canton, but only the unsatisfactory road connections through Kweichow. If, on the other hand, Chiang Kai-shek retreats south into Hunan, he will be in a strong military position with Canton and its munition imports at his back, but he will be out of touch with Szechwan and still more with Shensi and Kansu, so that the recently created national unity, depending so much on a centrally situated capital and adequate communications, will be gravely impaired.

If the Japanese are not diverted from China by a war with Russia, and if they can take Hankow, it seems likely that China will in effect be divided into three parts:

(1) The South, remaining under Kuomintang rule, with Canton as link with the outer world; primarily the three provinces of Kwangtung, Kwangsi and Hunan, with Szechwan loosely attached.

(2) The Northwest, under Communist rule, linked with the Soviet Union by the Lanchow-Urumchi road; Kansu and Shensi plus Ninghsia and Sinkiang beyond the Great Wall.

(3) The Northeast, including the Peiping-Tientsin, Shanghai-Nanking and Hankow areas; divided between Japanese-controlled governments and Communist guerrilla formations; Japanese occupation of chief towns and along the Yangtse and railway lines.

The war has already produced a curious reversal of roles between the North and the South. For several decades up to last year the South was, on the whole, a revolutionary force in conflict with the conservative North. Today the North is the stronghold of Communism, while the South is by comparison conservative. The Communists of Kiangsi, driven out by Chiang

Kai-shek in 1934, made a long trek through Hunan, Kweichow and Szechwan to Shensi[1] and there renewed their strength with a somewhat modified program; then, as a result of the famous kidnaping of Chiang Kai-shek at Sian at the end of 1936 the Kuomintang and the Communists came together in a national united front, the Communists adopting the national flag, but retaining in fact under their own rule the territory they held. After the outbreak of the war with Japan the Communist leader Mao Tse-tung was made governor of Kansu—a province vital for communication with the Soviet Union—and the Communists, alias the Eighth Route Army, took over the conduct of the war north of the Yellow River. The old Chinese administration in Shansi and Hopei having been broken up by the Japanese invasion, the Communist guerrillas have extended control over all the districts not actually held by Japanese garrisons. Thus, while the South remains more or less solidly attached to the Kuomintang, North China has become a battle-ground between the Japanese and their handful of ultra-reactionary Chinese followers on the one hand and the Communists with their mass-mobilization peasant auxiliaries on the other.

If Hankow falls, Canton will again be the main base of the Kuomintang, as it was before 1926. If Canton is lost, resistance can be continued in the mountainous Southwest with the railway to Yunnan from French Indo-China and the newly constructed road to Yunnan from Burma as routes of supply. But it is very unlikely that the Japanese will seriously attempt to capture Canton. Not only would it require a large expeditionary force, which Japan cannot afford to send out in addition to all

[1] For an account of the "Long March" see Edgar Snow, *Red Star over China*, part v.

her other commitments, and a landing on a wide front on a well defended coast; it would also almost inevitably involve complications with the British at Hongkong which all but the wildest of Japanese extremists desire to avoid, at least in the immediate future. The leased New Territory of Hongkong would greatly impede any operations against Canton, and "incidents" would be sure to occur along the border; the British reaction to these would be much sharper than at Shanghai, for not only is Hongkong British territory (which the International Settlement at Shanghai is definitely not), but it now represents the whole stake of British interest in China. While British trade in North and Central China has suffered eclipse as a result of the war, Hongkong has enjoyed a boom. The foreign trade of independent China is again concentrated at Canton, as it was before 1842, and Hongkong is Canton's open-sea port. The Japanese capture of Canton would put an end to this trade, and Britain has therefore the strongest of reasons for doing everything possible to keep the open door open here, even though Japanese sliding screens may impede entry at Shanghai, Tsingtao and Tientsin.

Chapter X

THE FAR EASTERN TROPICS

The region of the Far East to the south of China and Formosa, lying entirely within the tropics, contains a total of 117 million inhabitants divided between six sovereignties as follows:

State		Population in millions
Netherlands Indies		60.7
French Indo-China		23.2
Siam		14.5
U.S.A.: the Philippines		13.3
Britain: Malaya 4.4	}	5.2
Borneo 8		
Portugal: Macao 1	}	.6
Timor 5		
		117.5

It is not easy to fix a natural boundary for this region toward the east, but it is convenient to count the Netherlands Indies as a unit, including Dutch New Guinea, within the Far East, and to distinguish Australia, Australian New Guinea (Papua and the former German colony now under an Australian mandate[1]) and

[1] The administration of Papua, formerly under the British Colonial Office, was transferred to the Commonwealth of Australia in 1906.

all the Pacific islands east of New Guinea and the Philippines as "Oceania." The Pacific archipelagoes, however, are of great strategic importance for Far Eastern affairs in view of their actual or potential development as naval and air bases, and it should be noted that four of the states holding sovereignty within the region of the Far East also possess groups of islands in Oceania. Thus no study of the Far East can avoid some reference to the distribution of "territory"—if consisting only of coral atolls—in the vast ocean spaces between Asia and the Americas.

Japan holds three groups of islands taken from Germany in the Great War:[1] the Marianne (or Ladrone), the Caroline and Marshall Islands. The Mariannes continue southward the line of the Bonin Islands—which are reckoned an integral part of Japan—and lie mostly between latitudes 20° and 10°; the Carolines and Marshalls form a belt stretching for some two thousand miles east and west between 10° N. and the Equator. There are about three thousand islands in all, the great majority being uninhabited coral reefs enclosing lagoons, useless for productive purposes, but admirable as submarine or seaplane bases.

To the south and southeast of the Carolines and Marshalls is a belt of British Empire ownership in five sections from west to east: (1) Australian New Guinea, full sovereignty in the south (Papua) and League mandate in the north over former German New Guinea; (2) the Bismarck Archipelago, formerly German, now under Australian mandate; (3) the Solomon and Santa Cruz Islands, British; (4) Nauru, formerly German, now under

---

[1] See p. 66. The Pelew Islands were formerly reckoned as a separate group, but the Japanese have included them for administrative purposes in the Carolines.

British Empire mandate, exercised jointly by Britain, Australia and New Zealand; (5) the Gilbert and Ellice Islands, British. These areas are, as it were, in the front line relative to the Japanese island groups. Farther back, below lat. 10° S., are Australia itself, the New Hebrides (Anglo-French condominium), the Fiji and Tonga Islands (British) and Western Samoa (New Zealand mandate).

The main area of French possession, including the Tahiti, Marquesas and Tuamotu island groups, lies far away to the east; in the westerly Australia-Fiji region, however, France also has her share in the New Hebrides condominium and full ownership of the large island of New Caledonia, economically important as one of the world's principal sources of nickel.

The American empire in the Pacific pivots on the Hawaii group, which lies roughly in the latitude of Hongkong. The Hawaiian Islands have a total population of 368,000 and contain the large town of Honolulu and the first-class naval base of Pearl Harbor. To the north, in the latitude of Kamchatka, are the Aleutian Islands forming a curved chain to the southwest of Alaska. Far to the south are the islands of Eastern Samoa, adjoining British Tonga and the New Zealand mandate of Western Samoa. A distance of more than 2,200 nautical miles separates Honolulu from Samoa, but in this vast space of ocean are scattered the Central Polynesian Sporades and the Phoenix Islands; among the former the U.S.A. owns the island of Samarang, and among the latter (which, as a group, are British) disputes with Britain the title to the two small islands of Canton and Enderbury. A curious compromise has just now been reached, whereby the question of sovereignty is left in abeyance "for a protracted period of time" and each nation accords the

NOTE ON MAP 31

"First-class" naval bases are those which are capable of docking and repairing capital ships. Hongkong was a battleship base before the introduction of "Dreadnoughts," but has not been rendered first-class for modern conditions; this rank has passed to Singapore, where the base was completed in 1937. The U.S.A. has so far no first-class base west of Pearl Harbor, Hawaii, and Japan has none south of Sasebo in Kyushu. Cavite (Manila) and Mako are cruiser bases like Hongkong. The standstill agreement on fortifications and naval bases in the Washington Naval Treaty of 1922 was intended to reduce tension by keeping battle-fleets at safe distances from one another, and the three great naval Powers of the Pacific are still very widely spaced out from a strategic point of view.

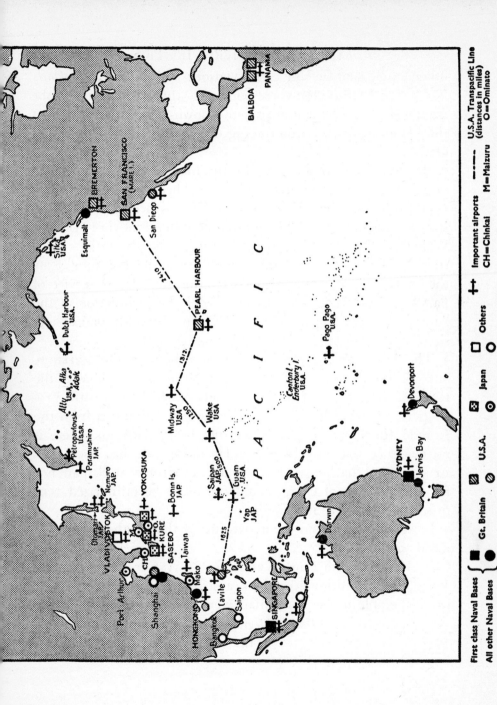

31. NAVAL AND AIR BASES OF THE PACIFIC

other equal facilities for civil aviation; according to the *Daily Telegraph* Washington correspondent[1] "there is nothing in the details of the settlement at present known which would prevent the [American] navy from taking over the islands in the event of war."

Between Hawaii and the Philippines lie three American-owned islands, not in a straight line, but breaking through what would otherwise be a three-thousand-mile space of sea containing only Japanese land. These three stepping stones are Midway, Wake and Guam. Before 1919 they were already stations for a trans-Pacific submarine cable, and during the last four years they have been in use as airports for the trans-Pacific service of Pan-American Airways. They are under the jurisdiction of the American Navy Department, and Guam, the only one of any size (225 square miles), is a regular naval station.

The American chain of islands cuts in between the Marianne and Caroline groups of the Japanese mandate. Under the terms of the League of Nations mandate, which Japan still professes to regard as binding, though she has withdrawn from the League, the Japanese islands may not be fortified, and there is no evidence that any large regular naval base has been constructed, but harbor works and an aerodrome at Saipan not far to the north of Guam could no doubt be militarized very quickly if war were imminent.

It will be clear from the above survey that in the event of a naval war in the Pacific,

(1) If the British Empire and the U.S.A. were allied against Japan, their position would be a strong one, and the U.S.A. would be able to use Australian New Guinea and neighboring

---

[1] *Daily Telegraph,* Aug. 11.

Australian or British islands for supporting American forces in Guam and the Philippines.

(2) If the British Empire were at war with Japan, and the U.S.A. neutral, New Guinea and Nauru (important for its phosphate deposits) would be exposed to attack from the Caroline and Marshall Islands.

(3) If the U.S.A. were at war with Japan, and the British Empire neutral, the Americans would have great difficulty in coming to grips with the Japanese in the western Pacific from their bases in Hawaii and Samoa owing to the great distances, while Guam with Japanese islands to north and south of it would be very insecure as a link with the Philippines until the Mariannes and Carolines had been entirely cleared of Japanese naval and air forces.

Such strategic considerations have a direct bearing on the political problems of the East Indies and Indo-China, for the question of the continuance or renunciation of the American control of the Philippines is crucial for that part of the world, and the position of America as a Great Power in the Far East depends on trans-Pacific communications. The European nations holding colonial territories in the Far East naturally maintain communication with them *via* the Indian Ocean and the Malacca or Sunda Straits; these lines cannot be intercepted by Japan. The line Hawaii-Manila, on the other hand, runs right across Japan's line Yokohama-Yap. The situation of the Philippines as a part of the American empire is so exposed that, in order to make sure of holding them in an era of imperialist struggle, the U.S.A. must in the long run either equip herself with armaments far in excess of what would be needed for the defense of the homeland and possessions as far as Hawaii, or must enter into defensive arrangements with other powers in the Far East. From the point of view of the European Powers with Far Eastern colonies the final departure of the Americans from the East Indies would be a great misfortune, for it would uncover the East Indies to Japanese expansion and leave the European colony-holders—who cannot deploy their full strength in the Far East as long as Europe is in a state of discord—to bear the brunt of it.

The Western Powers owning territory in the Far East have long since ceased to aim at further expansion or to contend with one another; they are concerned only to hold what they have, with the exception of the U.S.A., who is in doubt whether to retain or to abandon her rule. The Western Powers in the southern zone of the Far East are confronted today with political problems of two kinds: the first, that of dealing with the nationalist aspirations of the peoples under their sovereignty, and the second, that of preserving their territories from the expansionist aims of indigenous Far Eastern states—in which category must be included, not only Japan, but also Siam.

Among the hundred million Asiatics under Western rule in Indo-China and the East Indies three national movements are of real importance—the Javanese, the Annamese and the Filipino. Fully a third of the hundred million are entirely outside these three divisions, and they include the Indian and Chinese emigrant colonies, the Malays, the Khmers, the Balinese, the Bugis and a host of minor peoples and tribes. But in a brief survey it is possible only to take note of the three big aggregates numbering some forty, twenty and ten millions respectively.

Java and the scarcely detached island of Madura comprise

only a little over one-fifteenth of the area of the Netherlands Indies, but contain more than two-thirds of their total population, or 41.7 millions at 817.5 to the square mile. Java thus naturally forms the core of the Dutch East Indian empire, the rest of it being termed the "Outer Islands." Three languages are spoken: Sundanese in the west and Javanese in the east of Java, and Madurese in Madura. A "Javanese" may accordingly be either an inhabitant of Java or a speaker of Javanese, and in spite of the differences of language there appears to be enough common civilization in the islands for a Javanese nationality in the former sense to exist in fact. The "Indonesian" nationality, on the other hand, cannot be said to have any real basis; it exists only among a handful from various parts of the East Indies who have received a higher education in Dutch, and does not correspond to any popular consciousness. Outside Java and Madura insular and tribal particularism are so far too strong for the formation of any "Indonesian" unity, and the Javanese are as much foreigners as the Dutch; the Malay language provides a *lingua franca* on the coasts, but no adequate foundation for a coherent nationality, and Malay in any case cannot bind the Outer Islands to Java. The only vigorous nationalism is that of Java itself, but this is quite sufficient to confront the Dutch with a difficult problem of government.

The Netherlands India Constitution of 1925 granted a very limited measure of self-government in Java following the example of British concessions in India, but as the Indian example also shows, it is not easy to stop at any particular point on the road to "Dominion Status." The Dutch have no intention, as far as is known, of yielding up ultimate control over their East Indian empire, which has in the past been as lucrative as it has been easy to manage. But there has certainly been unrest in Java during the last decade, and there is always the possibility that a discontented element might seek foreign aid for a revolutionary movement. An independent Java might rapidly become a considerable power; it may be noted incidentally that the population of Java and Madura is six times that of Australia, and that Java, Borneo and Sumatra together form the most important oil-producing area in the Far East.[1]

In French Indo-China the ruling European Power has to deal with the growing nationalism of the Annamese, who form over 90% of the population of the territory. Unfortunately for France, the internal problems of French Indo-China are complicated by the proximity of an increasingly powerful and unfriendly Siam. The French colony[2] is composed historically of (1) the "empire" of Annam, including Tongking and Cochin-China, (2) the kingdom of Cambodia, and (3) territory taken from Siam, including Luang Prabang province and Battambang. Thus, while Annam and Cambodia were swallowed whole, Siam was merely mutilated, and today France, with a power depending on a small colonial force halfway across the world from the home country, is confronted with a modernized state which has a long history of wars and is now in the grip of an intense nationalism, has a population equal to that of Yugoslavia, is building up an army on a basis of universal military service, and has created a not negligible navy and air force. Siam in the 'eighties and 'nineties

[1] The oil production of the Netherlands Indies (of which about 97% comes from Java, Borneo and Sumatra) was 6,437,910 metric tons in 1936, and the country stands sixth in the world in estimated oil reserves.
[2] Formally only Cochin-China is a "colony," while Annam, Tongking, Cambodia and Laos are protectorates. But the difference is only that between French administration in Algeria and in Morocco.

of the last century only escaped the fate of her neighbors, Burma and Annam, because France and Britain could not agree on a division of the spoil and preferred to leave the country as an independent buffer state. Both Britain and France, however, helped themselves to outlying territories of the Siamese kingdom, and these losses are too recent to have been entirely forgotten in Siam.[1]

Another factor important in shaping Siamese policy is suspicion and fear of China on account of the large Chinese minority (2½ millions) in Siam. The Chinese formerly counted Siam as one of their "vassal states" on the strength of receptions of seal and calendar from Peking, and since the Revolution such historic claims have been brought up to date by spokesmen of the Kuomintang in the form of proposals for a future federal union of these states with China. Siamese nationalists reject the idea, and view any increase of China's power with apprehension, as they consider it is bound to have a disturbing effect on the overgrown Chinese minority and to compromise Siam's independence. They therefore tend to regard Japan's activities in smashing up the new Chinese state as extremely beneficial to Siam, and it was not without reason that Siam, alone among the attending members of the League of Nations, abstained from voting on the resolution of the League Assembly which condemned Japan's action in Manchuria in 1933.

Latent, but unassuaged, grievances against Britain and France and a strongly anti-Chinese bias have given Siamese policy in recent years an unmistakable pro-Japanese trend. Though the

[1] Britain in 1909 extorted the cession of Siamese suzerainty over the Malay principalities of Kedah, Kelantan, Trengganu and Perlis in return for partial revision of an extra-territoriality treaty.

rumors of a Japano-Siamese canal through the isthmus of Kra to short-circuit Singapore may be discounted—for such a canal would be as vulnerable in time of war as it would be costly to construct—Japanese influence in Bangkok has been strong enough to cause alarm to Britain and France, who have sought to deter Siam from such an undesirable friendship by imposing demonstrations of naval and aerial might. Measures of this kind may be effective for a while, but the attitude of Siam in the event of a European war would be determined by circumstances. In 1917 Siam declared war on Germany and seized German shipping and property in the country; Englishmen liked to think this was because the Siamese in the third year of the Great War had become convinced of the righteousness of the Allied cause. In another struggle of the European nations, however, Siam might decide differently on the question of right and invade French Indo-China with the assistance or collusion of Japan.

The position of French Indo-China between the Japanese navy and the Siamese army has suddenly become very dangerous, and the French have shown their awareness of the fact by a series of vigorous measures—increase of the military establishment, a "French Singapore" to be constructed at Kamranh Bay on the Annam coast north of Saigon, occupation of the strategically important Paracel Reefs southeast of Hainan, and warnings to Japan not to encroach on French vital interests by the seizure of Hainan in the war against China. But in the long run France's ability to hold Indo-China will depend mainly on the degree of her success in conciliating the Annamese; the latter have no desire to exchange one foreign yoke for another, but if there were enough discontent with French rule (and there has been a great deal), Annamese rebels might seek Siamese aid, the Siamese to take Cambodia and parts of Laos, which historically have a closer connection with Siam than with Annam.[1]

British Malaya is in a much less exposed situation than French Indo-China. It is relatively secure against a possible attack by land from Siam; by sea it is much more remote from Japan and is protected by the now completed first-class naval base at Singapore. Internally the political problems of Malaya are not too difficult from a British point of view. The Malays of the hinterland are divided among a number of small protected states, and in the Straits Settlements they are outnumbered by the Chinese and Indian immigrants, who have flowed in with the rapid economic development of the country. In these circumstances there cannot be any united nationalist movement and the classic formula of *divide et impera* is easily applied.[2]

Singapore is continually being developed as a seaport, airport and fortress on the assumption that Britain will endeavor to hold Malaya indefinitely, and France and Holland, closely linked with Britain in the triangle Singapore-Saigon-Batavia, show an equal resolve to stay where they are. In striking contrast with this dug-in attitude is the doubt at Manila about the intentions of the U.S.A. By an Act of the American Congress the Philippines are being governed for ten years from 1935 as a "Commonwealth" with an elected President and an American

[1] The Siamese national hero Phra Naret subdued Laos and Cambodia in the sixteenth century. The power of Cambodia had already been broken by Siam two centuries earlier.

[2] The government services have hitherto been reserved for Englishmen and Malays, but now the Chinese and Indians demand a share.

High Commissioner; in 1945 all American control is theoretically due to come to an end and the country is to become a sovereign "Philippine Republic." The abdication of American power was brought about in the States by an extraordinary log-rolling combination of anti-imperialist liberals, isolationists, sugar interests which wanted the Filipinos put outside the American tariff wall, and labor unions hostile to Filipino cheap labor immigration. The abdication appeared to be as definite as legislation could make it. Yet it may be considered improbable that the Americans will be out of the Philippines definitely in 1946.

Filipino nationality is of a peculiar kind. The group of islands called the Philippines had no sort of political unity before the Spanish conquest in the sixteenth century, and takes its name from a king of Spain. Further, the tribes of the Philippines (except in the extreme south) were converted *en masse* to Christianity—a phenomenon without parallel elsewhere in the Far East.[1] The nationalism of the Philippines has thus more similarity to that of Mexico or Peru than to that of Java, Annam or Japan, and the revolt against Spain in the 'nineties was largely inspired by Hispano-American examples. After 1898 U.S. American institutions and culture were superimposed on Spanish, and today both Spanish and English languages are current, the latter being the more widely known. But a nation cannot be quite happy with the language of alien conquerors, and so this year a law has been promulgated making Tagalog, the speech of central Luzon, the official language of the Com-

---

[1] The nearest analogy is provided by the Minahassa district in the northern peninsula of Celebes. But, generally speaking, Christianity has made little headway in the East Indies outside the Philippines.

monwealth. All this has caused considerable confusion; there are in fact a dozen vernacular languages of importance, and there are as many fair-sized island units outside Luzon. There is a strong Moslem minority known as Moros ("Moors") in Mindanao, and a Japanese colony, numbering about 14,000, engaged in the cultivation of hemp in the district of Davao in the southeast of the same island. On a broad view, the prospects of stability in an independent Philippine republic do not appear to be very bright; and when it is remembered that the most northerly island of the Philippines is visible on a clear day from Japanese Formosa, it is fairly obvious that the international position of the new state would be one of acute discomfort.

In Japan the program of overseas expansion toward the south is called the Nankai ("South Sea") policy. At its minimum this means nothing more than an intensified commercial drive, but at its maximum it implies a political ascendancy and the use of force. In its latter form, the Nankai policy is clearly an alternative to expansion on the mainland of Asia, and the debate between the Continental and South Sea schools is bound up with the professional rivalry between the two fighting services in Japan. In the opinion of the Japanese Army the Navy's function is to preserve Japan's communications with the continent and perhaps to harry enemy powers in war-time with commerce raiders, but not to set itself up as an independent force with a strategy of its own; the Navy's idea, on the contrary, is to restrain the Army from continental adventures, to avoid the liabilities of long land frontiers and to concentrate Japan's resources on building up sea-power. The bridling of the Army by the Navy was an evident fact when Admiral Okada was Prime Minister and Japan denounced the capital ship ratios of the

Washington Treaty. But the military mutiny of February 1936 ended Okada's rule, and the present war in China, even if it brings victory to Japan, must involve vast new permanent military commitments and reduce the Navy's share both of the national budget and of influence on national policy. The Navy's failure to prevent the new plunge into continental conquest may be attributed partly to the wider popular hold of the conscript army as compared with the limited personnel of the naval service, and partly to the fact that the Navy no less than the Army demands a large-scale autarchic heavy industry which can only be secured by control of North China.

Nevertheless the attractions of the Nankai program remain, and in certain circumstances it might again become practical politics. Malaya and Indonesia represent a vast market for cheap manufactured goods and also produce (or could produce) a great variety of raw materials, notably rubber, tin, oil and iron ore. British Malaya comes first, and the Netherlands Indies second, in the world's production of rubber; British Malaya stands first, and the Netherlands Indies fourth, in the world's supply of tin. The Netherlands Indies is the principal oil-producing region in the Far East; oil is found in Sumatra, Java, Borneo and the island of Ceram in the Moluccas. Finally, Mindanao in the Philippines and Celebes and southeastern Borneo in the Dutch domain contain vast deposits of lateritic iron ore, which are costly to work and have as yet been hardly touched, but which might in the future be of a great importance for a Far Eastern heavy industry. All these things, and especially the oil of Borneo and Ceram, might be objectives of Japanese expansion.

But the crucial question is whether or not the Americans

32. OIL, IRON AND TIN OF THE EAST INDIES

finally abandon the Philippines in 1945. If they go, it should not
be too difficult for the Japanese—unless they have suffered some
crushing disaster in the meantime—to gain control over the Filipino state and make it into a kind of Manchukuo, and with both
the Philippines and the Carolines in their hands they would
seriously threaten New Guinea, the Moluccas and eastern
Borneo at a safe distance from the Singapore base. If, on the
other hand, the Americans remain in the Philippines and keep,
under whatever juridical formula, a protectorate over the
islands, Japan will not be able to dominate the Philippines or to
invade New Guinea or the Moluccas across the Hawaii-Manila
line without risking war with the United States, and it is incon-
ceivable that she should do this as long as she has both Russia
and China as enemies on the mainland of Asia. The sole condition on which Japan would be likely to provoke the U.S.A. by
a South Sea expansion would be a Russo-Japanese *rapprochement*
giving rise to relations like those of 1907-17; such an appease-
ment would give Japan security on the mainland, so that she
could concentrate again on sea-power, but it is a possibility very
remote from the facts and policies of today.

If the Americans stay in the Philippines and continue to take
an active interest in Far Eastern affairs, a violent expansion of
Japan to the south or southeast is extremely improbable for a
long time to come. A frontal attack on Malaya across the South
China Sea is equally improbable. Hongkong and French Indo-
China, however, remain in a danger zone, for British and French
interests in access to China *via* Canton and Yunnan respectively
can at any time involve them in the struggle between Japan and
China which may continue, with intervals of truce, not for years,
but for decades. In this struggle the possession of Hainan is likely

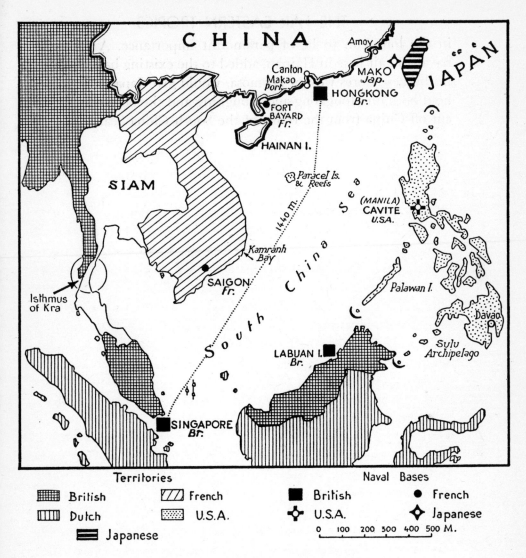

33. THE SOUTH CHINA SEA

in the long run to be of paramount importance. A Japanese naval and air base in Hainan, added to the existing base at Mako in the Pescadores west of Formosa, would give Japan a stranglehold both on Hongkong and Tongking and the power finally to cut off China from the traffic of the South China Sea.

SUPPLEMENT
THE FAR EAST, 1938-1942

By

GEORGE E. TAYLOR

With Additional Maps by
MARTHE RAJCHMAN

Chapter XI

THE UNITED STATES IN THE PACIFIC

The United States is not only an imperial power in the Far East sharing the interests of the western empires but also a Pacific power in her own right. She has therefore always had two distinct sets of relations, one with the western empires, sometimes co-operative and sometimes competitive, among them but not of them, and the other with the independent countries bordering the Pacific in particular, China, Japan and the eastern territories of Russia. The policies of the United States in this area have done more than is generally realized to determine, for a hundred and fifty years, the course of events in Eastern Asia.

The United States, from the territorial point of view, is necessarily pulled into Pacific affairs. In the north her Alaskan boundaries are separated from the mainland of Asia by a narrow sea. Japan is within flying distance of the nearest Alaskan bases. United States possessions in western Pacific waters, the South Pacific and the South China seas, rival those of any of the western empires; her naval bases lie much further from the homeland than do any of the Japanese; important airports extend from Dutch Harbour in the north to Pago Pago in the south, from Pearl Harbour in the east—itself 2410 miles from San Francisco —to Cavite in the west Pacific. The United States operates the only trans-Pacific air lines. The argument that America has been historically more interested in Europe than in Asia must take into account the fact that for decades she has held a position in the Pacific which she is only now, for example by the occupation of Iceland, beginning to acquire in the Atlantic. Whatever the apathy toward or ignorance of her role in America itself, there have been no illusions about her role in the Pacific among the countries in the Far East.

The policy of the United States has, indeed, been well defined and consistent. The ends of policy remain the same for all regions in which she is interested, the means by which policy is achieved derive from local and historical conditions. The United States has sought in the Far East, as in other regions, first and foremost the security of its own territories and the protection of its own nationals; for this reason it has a regional as well as a general interest in peace. A further end of policy is the development of economic interests and this naturally includes an active concern with the manner in which trade is conducted and with the maintenance of the economic principles underlying the American economy.

The main techniques which the United States has employed in the Far East to secure regional peace and its own interests are maintenance of a balance of power and freedom of the seas. Upon these depend the success of keeping an Open Door for commercial opportunity. These methods of handling Far Eastern affairs came into prominence at the end of the nineteenth century when the United States re-emerged in the Orient after several decades of quiescence due to the Civil War. It was a different United States and a different Orient. From the end of the 18th to the middle of the 19th century the United States joined vigorously in the expansion of European trade and methods of trading to the East, partly as a result of her commercial rivalry with Great Britain, partly because the merchant capital of New England found the clipper trade a far more profitable business than expansion across the American continent. The British command of the South China seas following the capture of Singapore in 1819, the development of the American Pacific coast, the growth of the whaling industry and the improvement in shipping led to the use of the Pacific route. Rivalry with Great Britain gave the impetus to the opening up of Japan. It was necessary, as Commodore Perry put it, to anticipate the designs "of that unconscionable government, the British Government" whose cupidity was limited only by its capacity to satisfy it.—"The honor of the country and the interests of commerce demand it." This was the language of a trading nation, but the United States which re-entered the Pacific scene in 1898 was a continental empire with vast industrial possibilities and growing accumulations of capital to invest. Revived American energies took United States commerce and investments into the Caribbean and Central America, a development forming the background of the Spanish-American War which led indirectly to the seizure of the Philippine Islands.

The age of British sea power in the Far East, or at least of British monopoly, waned as the 19th century came to a close and a new balance of power came into being. The building of the Trans-Siberian railway brought the Eurasian land mass of Russia into the picture and gave a land frontier on China outflanking British naval power; the defeat of China by Japan in 1895 changed the relation between these two Far Eastern powers. Completion of German and Italian unification in 1870 hastened the tempo of imperialist competition to such an extent that Africa was divided in twenty short years and pressures upon China became intense during the last decade of the century. Under such circumstances the only way in which the United States could trade in the Far East was by preserving the formal independence of China, her main arena of business, and this was possible only on condition that China was not divided. The revolt of China against imperialism at this time, the Boxer rebellion, in the suppression of which United States troops participated, helped to prevent the partition by compelling the powers to unite at the very moment when they were in violent competition. Because there was actually a balance of power it was possible for the Open Door to be accepted. No one country was strong enough to shut it.

The Open Door policy, as it is called, happened to be a technique best suited to the peculiar conditions of the time—it has never been a moral principle universally applied in all regions where American policy was active, or even in the Far East itself. But the natural corollary of this was the need to prevent China collapsing and thus endangering the balance of forces. The general purpose of American policy toward China has been to keep China in that state where she would be weak enough to take orders but strong enough to obey them; in other words, the United States was as active as any in maintaining those treaty rights which she shared with other powers, and which constituted a violation of Chinese territorial and political integrity, and intervened actively, for example, in the 1920's, when these rights were endangered, but was more willing than some to keep alive the goose that laid the golden egg.

It is generally true that when Russia became too strong the

United States supported Japan; when Japan became too strong support was given to Russia. The Anglo-Japanese alliance, devised mainly to counterbalance Russian imperialism, came in with an American blessing; it went out, when Russian imperialism was apparently dead, with an American curse. So long as the Chinese capital remained in Peking the pivot of American policy, the keystone of the balance of power, was Manchuria, and various schemes were suggested for making it a more effective buffer state. Manchuria fell to the Japanese in 1931 partly because it had already lost much of its meaning; the political center of China had moved to the Yangtse valley and the character of the international situation had changed. The theory that Japan was permitted to set up a bulwark against Communism must not be exaggerated because in the Siberian campaign of 1919 the mission of the American forces was concerned far more with the prevention of Japanese expansion than assisting the Czechoslovak legionnaires. From 1931 to 1941 the focus of the Far Eastern balance of forces moved south until finally it centered in the South China Sea.

The fact that the United States has only rarely used force in the Far East can be attributed less to unwillingness to use it than to her success in maintaining the balance of power.

At the same time the ratio of naval forces between Japan, Great Britain and the United States, together with the non-aggressive policies of the U.S.S.R., made possible a wide margin of action on the part of Japan before she endangered her relations with the Anglo-American empires to the point of war. This continental expansion and southward drive of Japan have called forth, on the part of the United States, expressions of policy which reflect the general purposes and techniques of that policy in new forms, but the essence remains the same. The institutions of the United States as well as her geographical position combine to support a desire for general peace, essential for the security of the nation, and to sublimate the balance of power policy into what Mr. Cordell Hull has called "order under law." From the American point of view there was a perfect combination of principle and interest in insisting upon the maintenance of treaty rights, both by China and Japan, upon the sanctity of international law, upon the refusal to recognize, at least in the Far East, changes brought about by force. While Franco's conquest of Spain was recognized, the spread of Japanese sponsored regimes was not, while American treaty rights on the high seas were abolished by Congress, in the Neutrality Act, the rights to extraterritoriality, to the stationing of troops and gunboats, and to administrative privileges, in China, were protected against all comers. Yet the maintenance of these rights, from the Chinese point of view, constituted a continuous infringement of the other American principle of concern for China's integrity. Nor was the Open Door open for China; none of the powers conceded to China the rights they demanded from her.

United States policy can be properly stated only if it is understood that most of the things which are usually called principles are really techniques, applied unilaterally to the Far Eastern situation. The language of Secretary Lansing in 1914 put the situation very frankly: "This Government will be glad to exert any influence, which it possesses, to further, by peaceful methods, the welfare of the Chinese people, but the Department realizes that it would be quixotic in the extreme to allow the question of China's territorial integrity to entangle the United States in international difficulties." In other words, the United States has been far less actively concerned about the integrity of China than has Britain about the integrity of Belgium and Holland, for the simple reason that it was of less concern to American interests. Statements of American as of British policy are more a guide, when they deal with principles, to the sort of world they would like to live in than to the motives which inspire action.

It is often overlooked that democracies, as well as dictatorships, spread their ideas abroad. The American government has quite naturally been active in the protection of its missionaries on the one hand and its own philosophy of economic behavior on the other. The effect of American ideas upon Japan and China has been impressive, in the latter case revolutionary. It is arguable, from the Japanese point of view, that the presence of American colleges, churches and business houses in China represents a political force as potent as the most active fifth column of the totalitarian states. Japan has everything to fear from the spread of American influence in China, in fact this is one of the things that she is most concerned to wipe out—hence the attacks upon educational institutions and the curtailment of missionary activities. American propaganda in the East is none the less potent for not being organized by government; its impact upon Chinese society is patent to all, and American consular and diplomatic agents have always used the missionary and businessman as a source of information. It is the success of this propaganda in China, as contrasted with Japan, which accounts for the sentimental stake that the United States has in China, and China in the United States.

United States policies in the Far East cannot be explained in terms of investments and trade. American investment holdings in China, before the "incident," amounted to only $240,000,000,

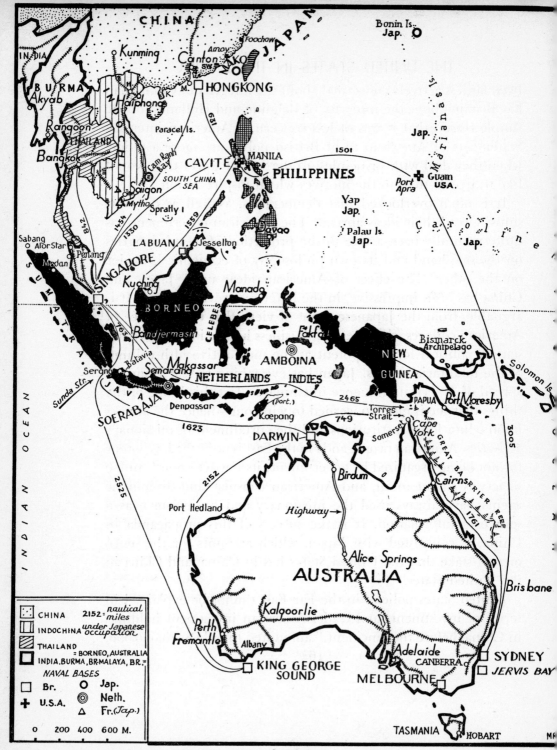

34. THE SOUTHWEST PACIFIC

her total trade to $250,000,000. For Japan the amounts ran about three times as high. As far as China and Japan are concerned the United States is interested in preserving opportunity for trade and the American way of conducting trade rather than in fighting for the preservation of investments as such; from the economic point of view she can afford to lose the battle for China and let Japan overrun it, as she has, but from the political point of view the old concern for China's so called "integrity" is important. The power that can control, if not exploit, China can challenge the whole balance of power in Eastern Asia and endanger the very important strategic and economic interests that the United States and others have in the South China Sea. It is the southward drive of Japan which most concerns the United States.

The change in United States actions in the Far East came after the fall of Holland and France. Up till then the flow of war materials to Japan had gone on without serious interruptions, the argument being that Japan was bound to expand and that as no one was willing, on general principles, to stop her, it was the better of two evils if she spent her energies on the continent rather than in Southeast Asia. So long as the raw materials for war which came from the trade with America were expended, and, it was hoped, wasted, in China there was no urgent reason to stop the flow, for the imposition of an embargo might well have turned Japanese energies in other directions. The U.S.S.R., which sought to prevent a Chinese collapse, and would have preferred Japanese oceanic expansion, supported China with arms and munitions and immobilized the best equipped sections of the Japanese army in Manchuria.

The effect of the policies of the U.S.S.R. and the United

States was the same, to permit the aggressive power in the East to weaken itself against the rising tide of Chinese resistance. Soviet trade continued with Japan although some pressure was put on Japan with regard to the fishing rights in Russian waters, and the United States continued to trade with China although insisting on the cash and carry provisions of the Neutrality Act.

The relations between the United States and Japan changed when it became clear that Japan had ambitions in Southeast Asia for here lay important interests. The most optimistic studies of the degree to which the United States depends upon the Far East for strategic raw materials admit that such materials as tin, rubber, abaca and quinine, if obtained elsewhere, would be in quantities sufficient only for immediate American military needs; even this depends upon the assumption that the sea lanes to the U.S.S.R., South Africa and South America remain open. New sources of supply, scrap, synthetic products, and substitutes can possibly replace these materials from Southeast Asia, but the replacements would be extremely costly and the changes involved would be very extensive involving, in some cases, a period of several years. Only the accumulation of large stocks could avert disaster while these measures were being taken. There are no climatic reasons why Far Eastern vegetable products could not be grown in the Western Hemisphere, but the high cost of labor prevents their production in the Western Hemisphere in peace time, and new plantations could not be made productive enough in sufficient time, during a war emergency, to be of practical value. Over 85 per cent of American rubber imports come now from British Malaya and the Netherlands Indies, a fact of enormous importance in war, for it takes between five and seven years to bring a rubber plantation into

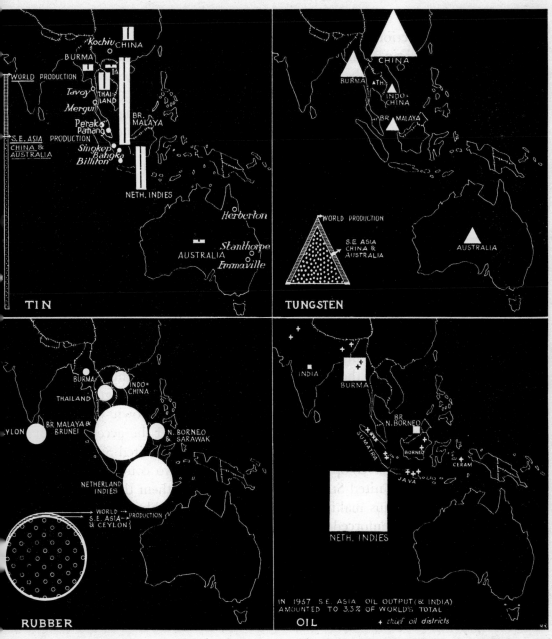

TIN

WORLD PRODUCTION

S.E. ASIA PRODUCTION
CHINA &
AUSTRALIA

Kochiu — CHINA
BURMA
Tavoy
Mergui
THAI-
LAND
Perak
Pahang
BR.
MALAYA
Singkep
Bangka
Billiton
NETH. INDIES
Herberton
Stanthorpe
AUSTRALIA
Emmaville

TUNGSTEN

CHINA
BURMA
THAI
INDO-
CHINA
BR. MALAYA
AUSTRALIA

WORLD PRODUCTION
S.E. ASIA
CHINA &
AUSTRALIA

RUBBER

BURMA
INDO-
CHINA
THAILAND
YLON
BR. MALAYA &
BRUNEI
N. BORNEO
& SARAWAK
NETHERLANDS
INDIES

WORLD PRODUCTION
S.E. ASIA
& CEYLON

OIL

INDIA
BURMA
BR.
N. BORNEO
SUMATRA
BORNEO
CERAM
JAVA
NETH. INDIES

IN 1967 S.E. ASIA OIL OUTPUT (& INDIA)
AMOUNTED TO 3.3% OF WORLD'S TOTAL
+ chief oil districts

35. STRATEGIC RAW MATERIALS OF THE SOUTHWEST PACIFIC

production. Scrap rubber to the amount of one fourth of the American demand can be reclaimed, but not used for tires; synthetic rubber can be produced at great cost, but at least a year would be necessary to expand production.

The United States, therefore, could not willingly permit the Netherlands Indies and the Malay Peninsula, the Philippines, south China and the south Pacific to fall into the hands of an unfriendly power, both because she depended on this area for vital strategic materials and because control of such materials would strengthen considerably the power of the enemy. It was a necessary part of American strategy that the Japanese drive to the south be stopped, a fact which became clear when Mr. Matsuoka, while in office as Japanese Foreign Minister, went out of his way to convince the world that Japan intended to give no more respect to the *status quo* in the Pacific.

The naval position of the United States in the Pacific had changed even before the armament program got under way after the fall of France. It had for years been assumed that in time of crisis the British and American fleets might well be acting jointly in the Pacific, for although the Washington conference gave Japan a favorable position in her own waters, the cancellation of the Anglo-Japanese pact and the acceptance by Great Britain of battleship parity with the United States paved the way for co-operation between these two countries. Britain and the United States controlled between them the exits to the Pacific, thus making possible a long range blockade of Japan, which, if enforced, would compel her to fight far from her own bases. But it was the ever lengthening radius of air power which gave the United States a potential advantage over Japan, especially after the abrogation of naval limitation treaties in 1936.

THE UNITED STATES IN THE PACIFIC

Guam, which had not been fortified as a naval base, became very important as a possible submarine and air base only 1,500 miles from Japan; the Aleutian Islands reach out to within 2,000 miles of Japan's industrial areas. The cancellation of the non-fortification agreement by Japan herself worked to the advantage of the United States; Japan had no territories within 1,500 miles of American shores. On the contrary, Japan's easternmost possessions in the Marshall Islands are still 2,000 nautical miles even from Hawaii and her nearest naval station is 6,600 miles distant from the Panama Canal. The United States, therefore, seemed to have control of the western and considerable power in the eastern Pacific. That the time was too short to develop these potentialities is a matter of history.

Full advantage of the treaty situation as regards naval power in the Pacific was not taken by the United States until the new armament program began in 1940 but pressure was applied, though very gently, in the economic sphere. The first step, the "moral" embargo of June, 1938, on exports to Japan of aircraft armaments, engine parts, accessories, aerial bombs and torpedoes practically stopped all trade in these categories. In December, 1939 the embargo list was extended to include molybdenum, aluminum, and equipment or information required for the production of high-quality aviation gasoline. In January, 1940, the trade treaty of 1911 was abrogated but not until the fall of France did Congress give the President authority to subject exports to a licensing system. Actions up to this time on the part of America can be explained as much by the restriction which Japan put on trade with the U. S.—for example, the two million dollar tobacco export to Japan fell to two thousand dollars in 1939 and to nothing in 1940—as by political motives.

171

Nor did the U. S. go out of its way to weaken Japan by giving decisive support to its enemies until the events of 1940 changed everything. A loan of $25,000,000, to be repaid in shipments of wood oil, was granted China in December, 1938, and one of $20,000,000 in March, 1940 to be repaid in tin; these loans were of political value to China, but in effect, the United States merely financed the importation of strategic materials.

The United States was well aware, as was pointed out in the note to Japan of December, 1938, that the situation had changed. "This Government is also well aware that many of the changes have been brought about by the action of Japan. This Government does not admit, however, that there is need or warrant for any one power to take upon itself to prescribe what shall be the terms or conditions of a 'new order' in areas not under its sovereignty and to constitute itself the repository of authority and the agent of destiny in regard thereto." But the United States did not feel it necessary to act until the whole basis of the world balance of power was shaken by the German offensive in the spring of 1940. Then came a crisis in American policy; for the first time in a century and a half of contact with the Far East the United States was faced with a situation in which it would have to defend its interests by the threat of full scale military and naval operations.

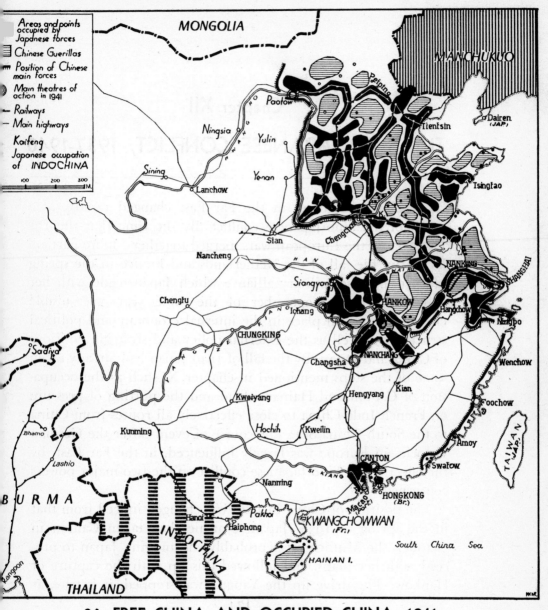

MONGOLIA

MANCHUKUO

Ningsia

Yulin

Peiping

Dairen (JAP)

Tientsin

Sining

Yenan

Lanchow

Tsingtao

Nancheng

Sian

Chengchow

NANKING

SHANGHAI

Siangyang

Chengtu

Ichang

HAN R.

HANKOW

Hangchow

Ningpo

CHUNGKING

YANGTZE KIANG

Changsha

NANCHANG

Wenchow

Sadiya

Kweiyang

Hengyang

Kian

Foochow

Bhamo

Kunming

Hochih

Kweilin

Amoy

TAIWAN (JAP.)

Lashio

BURMA

Nanning

CANTON

Swatow

Macao (Port.)

HONGKONG (Br.)

Hanoi

Pakhoi

Haiphong

SI KIANG

KWANGCHOWWAN (Fr.)

South China Sea

INDOCHINA

HAINAN I.

Rangoon

THAILAND

36. FREE CHINA AND OCCUPIED CHINA, 1941

Chapter XII

THE SINO-JAPANESE CONFLICT, 1937-1940

The balance of forces in the Far East changed rapidly as a result of the Sino-Japanese conflict. By the time that the Far Eastern and the European wars merged together—more particularly after the fall of the Netherlands and France in the spring of 1940 and the military alliance which Japan made with her Axis partners in September of the same year—measurable changes had taken place in the internal economic and political structures as well as the external policy and strategic positions of China and Japan. By the fall of 1940 Japan had already taken some of the steps mentioned in chapter X, such as the occupation of Canton and Hainan island and the putting of pressure on French Indo-China to close effectively all routes from China to the South China Sea. The course of events after the German victories in Europe was largely influenced, in the Far East, by the effect of the Sino-Japanese conflict on the two major powers concerned.

The position of China in 1940 was changed indeed from that in the spring of 1938. Japanese armies had taken Canton in October, the Munich crisis probably encouraging Japan to proceed with her plans, and followed this up with the capture of Hankow. The drive up the Yangtse was stopped, it is true, at

Ichang, and the push to the south did not reach Changsha, but the positions held by the Japanese in central China were sufficient to disrupt important Chinese communications and make the feeding of widely separated armies a major problem. The real turning point of the war, however, had come when China survived the loss of Nanking and by refusing to come to terms forced Japan to embark upon the annihilation of Chinese arms and government. By the winter of 1938-1939 the Japanese armies were fought to a standstill and since the spring of 1939 there have been few changes in the territorial distribution of the two opposing armies. Japanese strategy ceased, apparently, to consider the cost of further invasion worth the price in men and materials and the conclusion of the conflict was sought, from this time on, by other means. On the military side this was attempted by seeking to close all the gates that China still held open on the world, particularly those leading through French Indo-China, British Burma, and the remaining unoccupied treaty ports, on the political side by attempting to create an alternative government, in the occupied territory, to the Chungking regime, which Tokyo had refused to recognize since January 16, 1938. The stalemate in military affairs contributed, therefore, to the Japanese drive to the south and the increasing tension in Japan's relations with the western empires. In China itself the struggle for territory gave place to a struggle for government.

The military stalemate came about only in part as a result of the Chinese strategy of fighting the war in three stages—a stage of withdrawal, a period of stalemate, and finally, after Japanese exhaustion and Chinese preparations, counterattack. There is no question but that the Japanese invasion was made costly by the stubborn resistance of the Central troops at Shanghai and the operations of the guerrilla units behind Japanese lines in the north. China made full use of her territory as well as of her social and economic organization, which made this type of resistance possible. But the Japanese themselves are responsible for important contributions to the smooth working of Chinese strategy by failing to prepare those conditions necessary for successful blitzkrieg. Instead of dividing China they united its two most discordant elements, the Kuomintang and the Communists. Far from lulling China into a sense of security and encouraging lack of preparation they heralded the coming conflict by a series of declarations and actions which left no doubt of their intentions. The victim was not isolated by diplomacy or by previous encirclement, the way was left open for contact between China and the western empires and the U.S.S.R., and even the military advisers of Japan's ally, Germany, remained at their posts for most of the first year of war. Nor was sufficient allowance made, in terms of strategy, for the fact that China's communication system did not accurately reflect the economic complexity of her economy; strategy was based on the assumption that control of the cities and means of communication would bring with it control of the hinterland, which it did not, and time which could have been better spent in immediate occupation of the hinterland was spent in further advances into the interior. Almost every rule for successful war was violated, strategy and politics were at variance and diplomacy hindered rather than helped the progress of the armed forces.

The achievements of the Japanese army must not be lightly dismissed, however, by measuring them against perfectionist

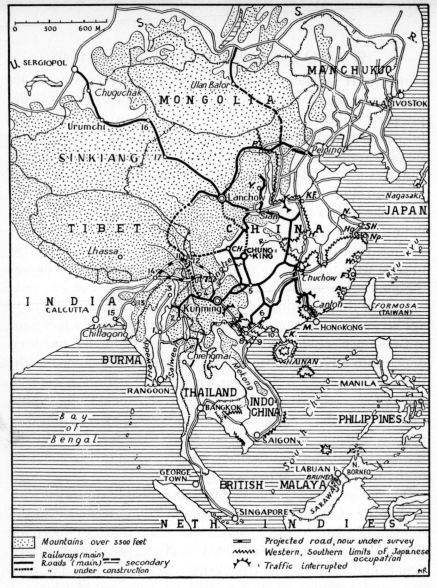

0	300	600 M

Mountains over 3300 feet
Railways (main)
Roads (main) **== secondary**
" under construction

Projected road, now under survey
Western, Southern limits of Japanese occupation
Traffic interrupted

HR

Numbers and letters on the map correspond to the following names:

1	Mandalay	11	Ningtsing	Hg	Hangchow
2	Lashio	12	Batang	K	Kwangchowan (Fr.)
3	Myitkyina	13	Silchar	Kf	Kaifeng
4	Tali	14	Sadiya	M	Macao (Port.)
5	Kweiyang	15	Dacca	N	Nanking
6	Nanning	16	Hami	Np	Ningpo
7	Ningyüan	17	Ansi	P	Paochi
8	Hanoi	A	Amoy	Sh	Shanghai
9	Haiphong	F	Foochow	W	Wenchow
10	Pachoi	H	Hankow	Y	Yenan

37. LAND COMMUNICATIONS IN CHINA AND EAST ASIA

standards. If Japanese armies were bogged down in China, Chinese armies were unable to drive them out of the country and the prospects of building up in the west the industry and materials for counterattack were no brighter than those of importing war supplies from other countries. Japan's flank, admittedly at great cost, was protected in case of southward expansion. China had lost control of most of her railways, important rivers, and highways; she had to watch the destruction of the major part of her industry, 80 per cent of which had been located in Shanghai; she was torn from her main sources of raw materials; she had to cope with the migration of millions of her people. Nor was the political front, which in many ways showed vast improvement over the conditions of 1937, entirely satisfactory, the cleavage between the Kuomintang and the Communists at times went as far as open conflict and in Nanking Wang Ching-wei had been drawn into a rival government under Japanese sponsorship. In those areas in which Japanese troops were stationed, control, except for occasional assassination of pro-Japanese Chinese puppets, went unchallenged. China's leaders were as determined as ever to continue the conflict but there were few signs, in the spring of 1940, to encourage any prospect of an early conclusion of the war on Chinese terms.

The lowest point in Chinese morale probably coincided with the closing of the Burma road by the British government in the summer of 1940. At the same time there was much to the credit side of the balance as far as China was concerned, for she more than held her own in the struggle for government. The Japanese sponsored regimes—the Provisional Government of China at Peking, established December 14, 1938, and the Reformed Government at Nanking, set up March 28, 1938, both later incorporated in the Reorganized National Government of China at Nanking under Wang Ching-wei, March 30, 1940—did nothing to aid Japanese arms. Mainly owing to the vigor of Chinese resistance, from the Border Government in the north, the Communist regions based on Yenan in Shensi, to the Kuomintang in Chungking, and partly owing to the political stupidity of the Japanese army, the puppet regimes failed to confuse, divide or attract the mass of the Chinese people or the leadership of free China. Free China has made it impossible for Japan to rule China indirectly through a Chinese regime founded on a sound social basis of classes favorable to Japan. Japan had to choose between leaving China to the Chinese or ruling it directly herself behind the façade of powerless puppets. In this connection North China was used as a kind of testing ground, for under the Provisional Government a new political party, the Hsin Min Hui, and a new political principle, the Hsin Min Chu I, were introduced to replace the Kuomintang and the San Min Chu I, and the flag of the Chinese Republic gave place to the five-barred flag. When Wang Ching-wei was installed in Nanking all this was dropped and the position assumed that Wang's government was the legitimate heir to the Chinese revolution, the orthodox as contrasted with the heretical branch at Chungking. The Reorganized Government at Nanking adopted, therefore, the San Min Chu I, the Kuomintang and the national flag. Nothing could illustrate better the political failure of the Japanese army, for this revealed that the only tactic left open to it was the attempt to divide Chinese leadership in Chungking by the offer of wealth, power, and personal safety at Nanking. Against these temptations the Chinese, in spite of bombings and hardships at Chungking, remained firm.

THE SINO-JAPANESE CONFLICT, 1937-1940

The building up of a new China went forward, during this period, on several fronts. That apparatus of the modern state which had been constructed in Nanking between 1928 and 1937, which constituted the Kuomintang's main contribution to China, survived the transfer from Nanking to Hankow and Chungking and in certain directions took on new forms and strength. China in 1940 had a national army, in some places a peoples' army, and had only the Japanese to thank for the destruction of provincial forces of the old type; she called the long postponed Peoples' Congress. Changes were made in the machinery of central government and in some districts an attack was made on the problem of modernizing local administration. Because the government depended, for ultimate victory, not only on the obedience, but also on the spontaneous co-operation of the people, the general effect of the war, there is evidence to indicate, was to encourage a closer relation between government and people and efficiency in administration. Out of the war came the impetus which brought forth the Chinese Industrial Co-operative movement, a form of association which gave promise of a broad basis for new social and economic patterns, tempering the necessarily authoritarian regulation of war time. Free China had to be a military agrarian state, for the army was the chief political force and agriculture, even more than before the war, the main part of Chinese economy; the government was the only body able to direct, control and invest in industry. The issue of the war revolved in large measure, therefore, around the question of political ends, whether they were to be democratic or fascist—the spirit that would inform the economic and social structure—and the outcome in 1940 was far from clear. The third stage of Chinese strategy, that of counter-attack, waited not only on materials of war and industrial growth, but also on the fusion of strategy with political and social ends.

Japan in the spring of 1940 bore many marks of change as a consequence of the war. The most obvious developments had come on the diplomatic front in the formulation of the New Order in East Asia, which later came to be extended to Greater East Asia. On November 3, 1938, Premier Konoye described Japan's ambitions as the establishment of a new order that would insure the permanent stability of East Asia and indicated that such purposes constituted the justification for the Sino-Japanese conflict. Vague as the statement was it came generally to be regarded as committing Japan to the destruction of Chiang Kai-shek's regime and the establishment of another government more amenable to Japanese desires, the elimination of "European Liberalism," that is, Anglo-American political, economic and social ideas, as well as the liquidation of the Western empires. This meant, in effect, the setting up of a Japanese controlled economic and political bloc from the Amur river to British Malaya and later, as ambition grew, to the Netherlands Indies and the Philippines. Japan extended its diplomatic front in a hostile world with friends but not allies, for the Anti-Comintern pact of 1936 meant nothing to her in terms of military assistance, and it was the unfavorable reaction which the New Order received in those countries which stood to lose most by it that assisted those Japanese who wanted to turn the Anti-Comintern pact into a military alliance.

The New Order for East Asia was balanced by a new order for Japan itself. The Japanese army soon took advantage of the war in China to pass through the Diet legislation to initiate *senji-keizai*, or full wartime economy. There is some debate as to the exact relation between the army and the big capitalists but it is clear that the very difficulties of the campaign in China did much to assist the military in securing the support of capitalists and bureaucrats. The General Mobilization Law of 1938 gave the government unprecedented powers over the whole of Japanese economy. The necessity of stabilizing the situation in China was again the chief argument used to justify the further movement towards the forms of totalitarianism of August 1940 in Konoye's announcement of the New Political Structure and the New Economic Structure. Through this the army achieved an old ambition, the abolition of political parties, for which were substituted an Imperial Rule Assistance Association. The membership of the new Association consisted largely of Konoye appointees. With this went the final step, in the New Economic Structure, of assuming complete control over industry, commerce, and agriculture. The nation had to be fully geared to the task of achieving, now, the creation of a New Order in Greater East Asia; it had taken the army from September 1931 to August 1940 to put itself in an unchallengeable position in Japanese life and commit the whole resources of the country to imperialist expansion.

The army influence upon Japanese economy was as far-reaching as its interference in diplomacy. The effect of mobilizing the armed forces in 1937 was to draw men away from production, and the need for re-armament tranferred men from agriculture to industry, a serious matter in a country where there is extensive application of human capital to the land. The need for armaments, naval and military, was greatest when the available man power was weakest. Production in agriculture, forestry and fishing went down; standards of consumption, after three years of war, were well under the already low levels of 1937; labor productivity suffered measurably from declining consumption. The production of producers' goods had gone up, of consumers' had gone down; Japan sacrificed butter but she had the guns.

Those in charge of Japanese policy were naturally those who least understood the impasse, diplomatic, economic and military, to which she had been brought. In this respect Japan was in a very different position from that of 1931; to say that her policies were now entirely subservient to the imperialist ambition of the military is the same as saying that decisions were not to be based on as careful an examination of the domestic and international situation as in earlier years. One of the most important factors in the whole development of Far Eastern affairs had now come to be the difficult internal position of the army; in order to maintain its domestic prestige serious changes had been made in Japanese politics and economics, changes which made it easier to form and to control opinion, but which did not make it any the less necessary to maintain public morale and keep up the prestige of the forces abroad. Even totalitarian states ultimately govern through opinion. In order to enslave East Asia the Japanese army first found it necessary to enslave Japan.

China in the spring of 1940 was compelled diplomatically to concentrate entirely on securing friends against Japan. Her position had changed, for Japanese occupation of the Chinese maritime provinces made the nineteenth century techniques of control meaningless; China no longer had her industry under foreign guns, no longer received the Maritime Customs revenues and had little to fear from extraterritoriality. For the time being the foreign settlements were China's chief outlets to the world and important centers of anti-Japanese activities. Japan, indeed, was

38. THE WESTERN PACIFIC

finishing one part of the work of the Chinese revolution by attempting to drive out western imperialism. China had changed, in other words, from a strong semi-colonial country at the mercy of foreign sea power to a weak though independent state based on the inner heart of her land mass. Japan, on the other hand, had lost much of her diplomatic freedom of action by committing herself openly to the destruction of the Western empires, by antagonizing the United States and by formal association with Italy and Germany. When the fall of France and Holland opened up new opportunities in Southeast Asia the direction of Japanese policy toward that area had already been prepared not only by the steps which followed the China war but also by earlier interests and policies in that part of the world.

Japan's commercial expansion in Southeast Asia and the south Pacific countries developed during the World War of 1914-18 and grew rapidly in the decade preceding the China war. Japan competed with advantage in a wide range of cheap goods, the most important being textiles, as against the more highly priced European and American products. During the first half of the thirties, it is asserted, Japan assumed a position of major importance in the commercial life of this area. The expansion of her export trade led to greatly increased imports of raw materials from the very countries which bought her goods. With goods went retail merchants into Thailand, the Netherlands Indies and the Philippines, where they competed with long established Chinese commercial groups. Nor was Japanese capital inactive in this region. Japanese rubber plantations, in which some 36 large firms were interested, produced around 20,000 metric tons of rubber a year as early as 1934. In Davao, southern Philippines, some 18,000 Japanese worked on Manila hemp plantations in 1939.

Japanese agricultural investments in the islands were estimated at $16,500,000; the big Japanese houses, such as Mitsui, Mitsubishi, Nomura, Okura, had built up interests in almost every product of the tropics—tea, coffee, cinchona; Japanese mines in British Malaya produced more than a fifth of Japan's total iron ore imports in 1937; Japanese sources estimate total investments in the mines, plantations, forestry, fisheries, and commerce of Southeast Asia and the South Pacific at about 250,000,000 yen.

The growth of this vested interest took place mainly in the colonies of Europe, of Great Britain, France, the Netherlands and Portugal, and partly in the American Philippines. It developed in spite of restrictions imposed by the controlling powers, which, after the conquest of Manchuria, began to fear that the Japanese flag would follow Japanese trade. A vicious circle appeared; increasing fear of Japan led to greater restrictions and greater restrictions to increased Japanese irritation, and in certain quarters, more sabre rattling. More important than this, however, was the financial strain of the war in China and the use of foreign exchange resources for munitions of war, which reduced Japan's capacity to purchase raw materials from this region for peacetime industries and therefore reduced exports and foreign exchange.

The effects of the China conflict became more and more far-reaching. If Japan had not embarked upon that adventure she would not have required so desperately the raw materials of war from the south at a time when she had less and less foreign exchange to purchase them with. The effect of the war was to make it more and more imperative for Japan to include her neighbors to the south in a yen bloc and to secure political control over raw materials which she had helped to develop under foreign flags. The southward expansion of Japan, which had been mainly an economic movement, turned into a political and military development in 1940 more as a consequence of the China war than of the developments in Europe which orphaned the colonies of two western empires; it was the opportunity which created the means.

39. SOUTHEAST ASIA

Chapter XIII

FAR EAST IN WORLD POLITICS

The role of Holland in the Pacific has been in some respects similar to her role in Europe—that of a weak power controlling very important strategic areas. No great power in the Far East could permit any other great power to dominate the rich raw materials, the cheap native labor and the strategic position of the Dutch East Indies, but Holland could be left in this position because she was not strong enough to oppose the policies of the powers or to change the general method of doing trade. The Netherlands Indies were in this sense the pivot of the Far Eastern balance of power; they were the Lowlands of the Pacific. When Holland and France fell, therefore, the impact was felt immediately in the Pacific.

The first world war began in Europe and spread to the rest of the world; the present conflict began in the rest of the world and finally reached Europe. In this sense the Far Eastern conflict has from 1931 been a part of the world struggle, though generally unrecognized as such—indeed the theory that seems to have been followed was that the European conflict might be avoided if the smaller fires were isolated and allowed to burn themselves out. The great system of Anglo-American-French domination of the world depended, in one aspect, upon maritime control of the industrial revolution, in the sense that none of the Great Industry could be permitted to develop too far out of the range of naval operations. The blockade was the chief weapon against land powers with the Great Industry. The most important and the first blow struck at this system, or this relation between land and sea power, came through the spread of the industrial revolution in the U.S.S.R., the second blow came through the development of air forces, the new power these gave to land armies and the new possibilities they opened up for the prevention of naval operations through narrow straits or near unfriendly shores. It was these things which made possible a battle for the world.

The Sino-Japanese conflict was from its very inception, therefore, a part of the larger struggle, the struggle to break down the domination of the world and its industrial development by the United States, Great Britain and France. Gaping holes were punched in the political structure of this world domination by Japan's invasion of Manchuria, by her withdrawal from the League of Nations, in company with her friends in Europe, and by the destruction of the treaty structure of the Pacific. If the fact of an Axis strategy be admitted, the Sino-Japanese conflict might well be considered as part of the "softening up" process in the struggle to destroy the world order. Certainly, when France and Holland fell, the merging of the Far Eastern conflict into the general European struggle became clear for all to see. Tokyo was not compelled to join the Axis by pressure of the United States or by a common interest in destroying communism, she joined the Axis only after the military had taken over full control of Japanese policies—here again the importance of the Sino-Japanese conflict, which helped to bring this about, is apparent —and after German diplomacy had succeeded in persuading the military diplomats of the ease with which the Anglo-Saxon powers could be destroyed and the world divided, to the advantage of Japan in the Pacific, among the conquerors.

The German successes of the spring of 1940 naturally strengthened the hands of those Japanese, such as the ambassadors to Berlin and Rome, who had earlier made an unsuccessful attempt to bring Japan into close relations with the Axis. The importance of the political changes in Japan in the summer of 1940—the establishment of the New Political and Economic Structures, and the destruction of political parties—became apparent in September, when the new foreign minister, Mr. Matsuoka, signed the military alliance of Tokyo with the Rome-Berlin axis. This alliance formally drew together the wars in the East and the West; it provided, in effect, that if the United States should extend its participation in either conflict beyond measures "short of war" then the other members of the Axis would engage in war with the United States. The intention of the pact, apparently, was to prevent the United States from acting decisively on the Atlantic front, in behalf of Britain, by threatening it with war in the Pacific, and to discourage American opposition to a Japanese attack on the Netherlands Indies by committing Germany, in such an event, to war with the United States in the Atlantic. Each member of the Axis, however, was left free to determine what constituted an act of war by the United States.

The next step in Japanese policy was to exploit the pact in her relations with the U.S.S.R. and the announced task of the new Japanese ambassador to Moscow, Mr. Tatekawa, was the conclusion of a non-aggression pact. Japan had much to gain if the U.S.S.R. could be persuaded to guarantee the Manchurian frontier, and reduce its supplies to China, thus permitting not only a conclusion of the China incident but also expansion to the south while the U.S.S.R. and the United States were both immobilized by the pact. Germany had made it clear, after the fall of Holland, that she was not interested in the future of the Netherlands Indies. German good will in the south was shown, moreover, by the pressure put on Vichy to accede to Japanese mediation in the border dispute with Thailand. Acceptance of Japan's demands on Indo-China in the summer of 1940 gave Japan supervisory rights sufficient to close Indo-China as a route through which supplies could go to Chungking, air bases from which she could reach the Burma road, and an opportunity for further embarrassing the colony by getting it into conflict with Thailand, over which issue she not only mediated but secured base facilities at Saigon and other points. If Japan appeared to have profited little as a result of the changes in Europe it must be remembered that Britain had not yet fallen, the attitude of the U.S.S.R. was uncertain, the Chinese were undefeated, the United States had gone out of its way in April, 1940, to point out that its policy in the Pacific was based upon respect for and maintenance of the *status quo*. The establishment by Tokyo of the Wang Ching-wei regime, March 30, had been followed twenty-four hours later by announcement of American loans to China and in June by a licensing system on exports to Japan. Perhaps the most important reason, however, why the Japanese did not strike immediately after the fall of France was that opposition in Japan itself had first to be fully overcome and that this took most of the summer. By the time that Japan had completed her internal changes the forces opposed against her were much stronger than those she would have faced in June.

The Japanese ambassador's mission to conclude a non-aggression pact with the U.S.S.R. was brought to a successful conclusion by Matsuoka in Moscow on April 13, 1941. The Axis military alliance of September did not affect the political status of each of the three parties with the U.S.S.R., it was up to Japan to get what terms she could. The pact, which runs for five years, guarantees friendly relations and respect for the territorial integrity of the two parties, and the one is to be neutral in the event the other is attacked by a third power.

The promise to respect the territorial integrity of the Mongol People's Republic and the state of Manchukuo merely regulated the *status quo* and was intended to remove boundary disputes as a source of friction between the two countries. The pact did not apparently include any agreements on the rest of China, and Moscow assured Chungking that supplies would continue as usual. It is difficult to see what Japan got from the pact, except the regularization of her relations with the presumed friend of the Axis, and a somewhat more favorable atmosphere for the settlement of problems such as Japanese fisheries rights, boundaries and trade. The U.S.S.R., in spite of respecting the territorial integrity of Manchukuo, did not cease aid to China or remove troops from Siberia. It is probable that Moscow knew in April that Germany was preparing to strike very soon and wished to prepare for Japanese neutrality as well as to encourage Japan to strike south and thus bring the United States and Britain into the war in the Pacific.

The United States, after the Japanese threat to extend its New Order in East Asia to Greater East Asia was noisily announced in Tokyo, very rapidly revised its whole strategy in the Pacific. The aim of her policy, to prevent a Japanese absorption of the lands to the south, was implemented by a series of moves which were calculated to more than achieve that purpose. A new attitude toward the U.S.S.R. became apparent in 1940 and early 1941, the United States apparently attempting to be friendly enough with Moscow to frighten Japan but not so friendly as to force Japan into the arms of the U.S.S.R. Mr. Oumansky, Soviet ambassador to Washington, had conversations with Mr. Welles, the Assistant Secretary of State, gestures were made such as permitting $7,000,000 of machine tools which had been held up on the Pacific west coast to proceed to Vladivostok. Secondly, assistance to China, now an important friend on Japan's flank who must be given the means to counter-attack in case of Japanese southward expansion, immediately increased, in fact, the United States very soon committed itself to assisting China through the Lend-Lease Act on a scale sufficient to guarantee her continued resistance. Prevention of a Sino-Japanese peace became of supreme importance to Washington.

Thirdly, the United States assisted the Netherlands Indies in defense preparations and by agreements with Great Britain and Australia enlarged the facilities for the U. S. fleet in the South Pacific. In April, 1941, there were Anglo-American-Dutch talks in Manila which, although secret, strengthened the impression that the three powers had plans for the joint defense of their interests in Southeast Asia. Australia and New Zealand were to contribute to the defense of the South Pacific and Australia in particular was a potential industrial hinterland for the defense of Singapore. Fourthly, the United States put pressure on Japan in such a way as to embarrass her war effort yet not, it was hoped, to force her into such a desperate situation that she would be compelled to fight. The effect of American economic measures up till

the complete cessation of trade in late July of 1941 was considerable.

Fifthly, the United States began to build up around Japan a
ring of air bases with long range bombers which was expected to
discourage any aggressive action against the South China Seas.
These bases extended from Alaska to Pago Pago, from Hawaii to
Guam and Cavite; in particular, the naval base at Pearl Harbor
was greatly strengthened and new naval facilities were built in
Alaska. The importance of small outposts in the Pacific, even if
not fortified as naval bases, becomes apparent now that air power
is of such importance in all military operations.

Most important of all, the United States, by including Great
Britain and her allies, and China, in the scope of the Lend-Lease
Act, showed that she considered the Far Eastern conflict to be
part of the European struggle; there was but one front but many
theaters of action. Nothing contributed so much to the new
orientation of American policy as Japan's adhesion to the military alliance with the Axis. If the Japanese really hoped that this
pact would act as a deterrent upon the United States they were
very disappointed; the attempt to force Washington to determine the extent of its intervention in Europe by threats in the
Pacific was too clumsy to succeed. There was no more effective
way of making the New Order in East Asia unpopular in America than by linking it up with Hitler's New Order in Europe.
If Japanese policy hinged upon the Axis, as Matsuoka told the
American ambassador to Japan, then Japan was bound up with
powers which are out to destroy the British Commonwealth and
Empire, whose survival the United States had decided was necessary for its own safety. Without the consent of the United States
there could not be a Japanese New Order in East Asia. Mr.

Matsuoka, by his alliance with Germany and then with the U.S.S.R., did more to align the democracies against Japan in one year than did the continental expansion of a decade; the first was, indeed, a logical consequence of the second.

The position of the U.S.S.R. during the course of the European war is clearer now than it was before the German invasion. The U.S.S.R. and Germany concluded an armed truce rather than a non-aggression pact in 1939 and the U.S.S.R. conducted its negotiations with each member of the Axis independently. The military alliance between the Axis powers, in September 1940, was discounted as the regulation of relations already existing between them but mention was made, in the Soviet press, of the spread of the war to include both East and West. Most important were Russian relations with China. From the very beginning of Chinese resistance to Japan in 1937 the U.S.S.R. has sent military supplies to China to assist in what the Russians look upon as a war of national revolution against an imperial power. No strings seem to have been attached to this aid, which went direct to Chungking and not to the Communist 8th Route Army. This aid continued even when relations between the Kuomintang and the Communists reached the breaking point and it continued in spite of the non-aggression pact between the U.S.S.R. and Japan. A Chinese-Soviet trade agreement was signed in January 1941 at a time when the New Fourth Army was being suppressed by Chungking. The Soviets have apparently been more concerned with Chinese independence and capacity to continue the struggle against Japan than with assisting the Communist movement in China, although the two are not unconnected.

Conflict between the U.S.S.R. and Germany changed once more the whole balance of forces in the Far East. Japan naturally

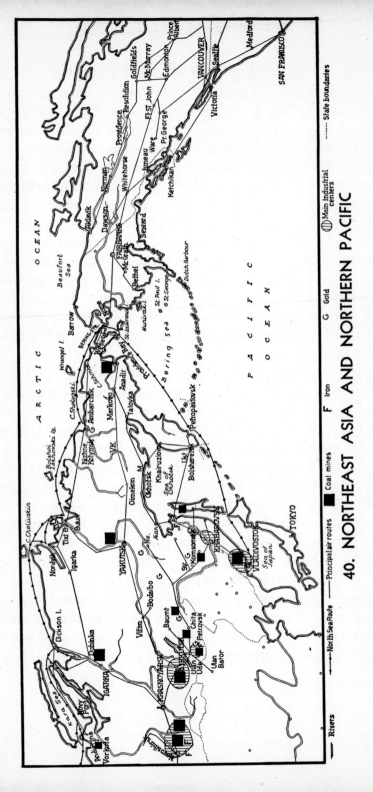

40. NORTHEAST ASIA AND NORTHERN PACIFIC

Rivers ——— North Sea Route ———→ Principal air routes ------- State boundaries

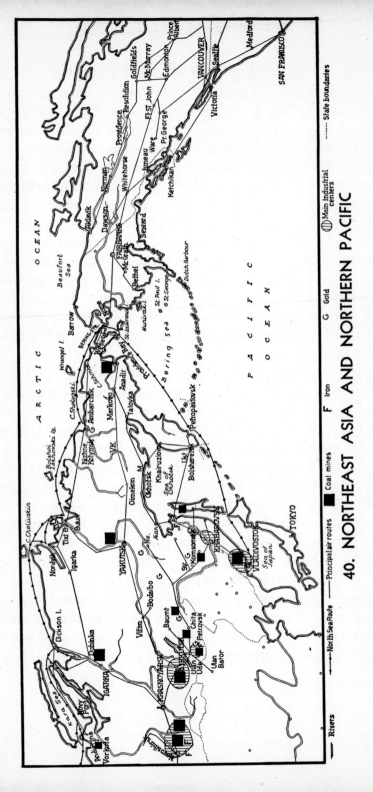 Main industrial centers ■ Coal mines F Iron G Gold

gained from any weakening of the Soviet Union and could assume that so long as the Russians were occupied in Europe they would not make any aggressive move in the East. Japan also gained by the stopping of Russian supplies to China. At the same time Great Britain was given a breathing space which it used, not to reinforce its positions in the Pacific, but to organize the Libyan offensive. The British hoped to keep Japan out of the war and were reluctant to take any steps which would "provoke" Japan into attack. The United States was equally anxious to prevent the struggle from spreading to the Pacific but fully realized that the matter had now resolved itself into a race between American military preparations and Japanese aggression. The deciding factor was the fortunes of war in Europe—the more the Russians retreated the more certain became the prospect of further Japanese aggression.

Relations between the United States and Japan steadily deteriorated. On July 25, 1941, freezing orders stopped all trade between the two countries and incidentally assisted the finances of China. It is true that Japanese-American conversations got under way in September between the highest officials of both countries, but they broke down. They were resumed by the special Japanese envoy, Mr. Kurusu, who flew to Washington to assist Admiral Nomura. In Japan itself a change of cabinet brought General Tojo in as prime minister and the military came out into the open as the directing political force. The composition of the Cabinet pointed to war. That Mr. Kurusu was sent to Washington merely to gain time and keep alive in America the hope of a peaceful solution is now quite clear, for the preparations for the attack on Pearl Harbor must have been in an advanced stage when Mr. Kurusu was on his way to the United States.

Mr. Kurusu's argument in Washington ran roughly as follows: If this comes to war you will probably defeat us in the long run, but you will have to exert every ounce of your strength to do it. At the end of the war you will occupy positions in the Southwest Pacific and China but you will have on your hands a state of anarchy such as we now have in China and you will not be able to get anything out of your conquests. It is not worth your while to stop us—it is much cheaper to let Japan have the Far East and you stick to the Western Hemisphere.

Such an argument could not be accepted. In the first place a Japan in control of Southeast Asia would be far too strong—she would have all the raw materials lacking in her own territories and the basis upon which she could build a very strong industrialized empire. America would have bought not peace but war —war on a much larger scale and without allies, if she had accepted the Japanese proposition. Secondly, the American intentions towards Asia were assumed by Mr. Kurusu to be similar to the Japanese, which they are not, and at the end of the war there would be no problem, for America, of preventing "anarchy" in China or elsewhere. Mr. Kurusu implied that America do to Latin America what Japan was about to do to Asia—a course which would have suited Japan's purposes very well, for it would have given Japan time to consolidate her empire and have involved the United States in a costly war in the Western Hemisphere. America could not accept those terms and Japan could not afford to let pass the golden opportunity for war—never again would come a situation in which the "confusion" of Europe would be matched by the "confusion" of America and the weakness of the Soviet Union. It was a choice, for Japan, of striking now or of waiting until the growing strength of America made aggression too costly.

FAR EAST IN WORLD POLITICS

For the United States it is historically fitting that she should have entered the world conflict by way of the Far East. It is in the Far East that the United States has always been the more deeply involved. In Asia the United States has had a position of leadership from which she could not abdicate, in Asia she has made every effort to spread her ideas and institutions. From rivalry with the British she passed to open ideological conflict with the U.S.S.R.; now she is locked in struggle with Japan to determine what political, social and economic concepts shall prevail in eastern Asia and the Pacific. There can be no compromise—the monopoly imperialism of Japan admits of no rivals and no competition. There is no solution of Pacific problems until Japanese imperialism is rooted out of Japanese society.

America entered the conflict at the last possible moment and with the maximum number of allies. She entered it in alliance with the western empires, with the Republic of China, with the Philippine people, with the U.S.S.R. fighting the chief ally of Japan in Europe. She entered the conflict at a time when the subject peoples of Asia were no longer indifferent to their fate, when nationalist movements were strong, and when the East had had ten years to contemplate the meaning of Japan's program of Asia for the Asiatics. The cooperation of the subject peoples, especially of India, is indispensable to victory, and they have already been predisposed in favor of the United Nations by the Japanese themselves. But the full mobilization of their resources and man power can come only through a realistic acceptance of their political aspirations for national independence. Here the importance of China as an ally is of overwhelming significance—China can furnish the biggest land front against Japan, especially against Manchuria, a vital industrial base, she can give enormous man power to the allied forces, and she can also stand as the greatest political factor in the struggle. So long as China is kept in the fight the subject peoples of Asia will have hope of eventual victory and freedom; so long as China fights, the claim of the Japanese that they are leading Asia will stand out as a hollow sham. China is the key to the New Pacific.

INDEX

N.B. *The plain numbers refer to pages, numbers after M to maps*

INDEX

INDEX

INDEX

INDEX

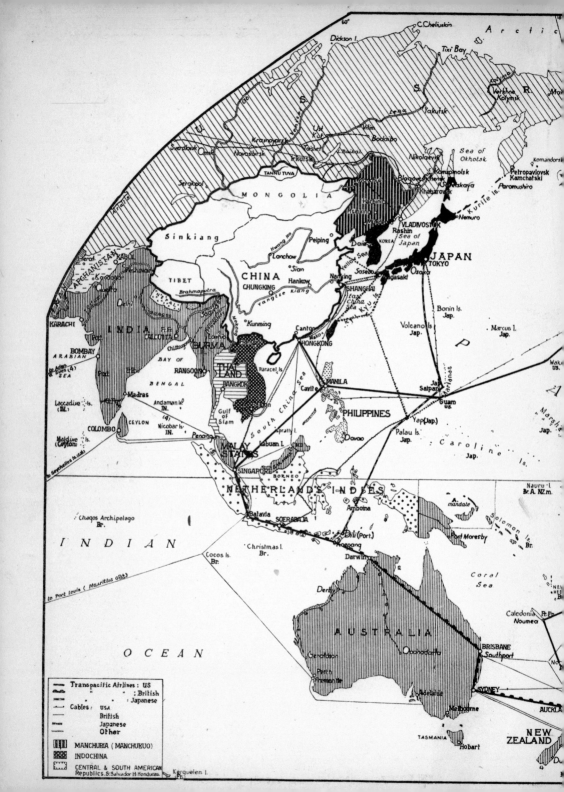